PLANES, TRAINS, AND WAR GAMES

A Fleet Air Arm Pilot's WWII Memoirs

J.A. Shipperlee
Anthea Gillian Tripp

TABLE OF CONTENTS

DEDICATION

Tony's beloved wife of 71 years

Phyllis Beale Shipperlee

Through the good times, the downtimes,
and all the in between times, she was by his side.

She was the wind beneath his wings

ACKNOWLEDGMENTS

A huge thank you to the love of my life! Chuck Tripp, you are my husband, best friend, business associate and so much more. You are the North on my compass, the wind in my sails, the music that makes my heart sing, you are my forever and ever love. You are my biggest writing fan, and your encouragement has meant the world to me as I compiled these memoirs. You brought me cups of tea and knew just the right timing to guide me away from the computer to stretch my legs and take a breather. You never complained about the many hours I chained myself to the computer, engrossed in the past! Thank you for always being there for me. Doing life with you brings me the greatest joy. Every day with you is a gift.

I owe a debt of gratitude to my son Stephen and daughter Chandra. You two rescued me from stagnating at the computer for days on end. After typing some of my father's stories, I could see many moons would pass before I would complete them all, which would delay me writing the expansion chapters. I think you know my typing skills leave much to be desired, with typos galore. Stephen and Chandra, you threw yourselves on the proverbial sword for me, and I am eternally grateful. Thank you for volunteering to take your Grandad's story drafts and use your superior skills to accurately retype thousands of his words and an abundance of complex military terminology into legible MSWord documents. You are amazing! Your help saved me endless hours of tedious work and enabled me to focus on writing the expansion chapters, thus speeding up the entire book process. Thanks a million. I love you both so much.

When I asked son David to edit the first draft, I knew he would find some typos I overlooked, and I also expected him to find some grammatical corrections, as he had always excelled at the English language, and it is a fact that writers can never catch ALL their mistakes—it's a given! However, I hadn't expected a full-blown professional style edit! David, you amaze me. You jumped at the invitation to edit the manuscript and by golly you took the task seriously and you did it full justice. You took editing to the next level, not only by catching typos, misspellings, and grammatical errors, but by offering fresh insight and thoughtful ideas—from which I was able to further enhance the manuscript. Thank you, David, for your editing skills and creative thought. Your help has effected changes that make the book a more meaningful and enjoyable experience for readers. I love you so much.

I could not publish this book without acknowledging David Stewart, who is my father's longest and dearest living friend—someone we accept as a member of the Tripp Family. He and my dad were the closest of friends and confidants, and for as long as I can remember, David and his family featured prominently in our life. I consider him an uncle, and I am so grateful to him for the lasting friendship with my dad and our family. When David and I talk on the phone he always mentions my dad and often reminds me *"we were the best of buddies you know, and I really miss him."* David, I am so grateful for your insight and input regarding my father. Thank you for answering the numerous questions I posed regarding who he was as a young man right after the war. You confirmed facts about WWII, assured me when I felt unsure of my suppositions, you filled in a few gaps, and illuminated parts of his life and actions that seemed unclear. Thanks for always welcoming my calls and indulging my many questions, I am grateful for your kindness and wisdom, and how generously you continue to reassure me of how proud my dad would be to know I have finally compiled his memoirs into book form. Your love and approval mean the world to me. Thank you from the bottom of my heart.

ABOUT THE AUTHORS

J.A.Shipperlee (Tony) was an educator, an artist and a WWII veteran who served as a pilot in the Fleet Air Arm branch of the British Royal Navy. He was an articulate writer and an accomplished storyteller who penned accurate accounts of his wartime experiences which are the source material in the book entitled Planes, Trains, and War Games.

Anthea Gillian Tripp is Tony's daughter. She wrote the expansion chapters in Planes, Trains, and War Games to add backstories to Tony's writing. In 2019, Anthea published her first book, My Soul Sings for You and writes passionately about the Life and Times of Now in her Blog at AntheaTripp.com. She co-owns Get Super Healthy, a health and wellness business.

INTRODUCTION
(Anthea)

As I stood in the reception line inside the church hall, following my dad's celebration of life, I struggled to overcome a flood of conflicting emotions. Dad had enjoyed an incredible ninety-seven years of life, lived on his terms. During that time, he had accumulated a multitude of friends and admirers many of whom attended his funeral. One friend after another, in quick succession, expressed their heartfelt condolences for my loss as they shared personal encounters that had endeared my dad to each of them. Some of them who knew him well shared their hopes that I would publish his WWII memoirs. I was grateful for each interaction, and the unanimous outpouring of admiration for the man they knew as a friend, neighbour, mentor, client, customer, or Fleet Air Arm veteran. A few knew him only in passing—as the "stooped old gent" from Bridge Street.

The man I call Dad.

My father was a familiar and highly respected figure in the Dorset community of Sturminster Newton, and those who knew him treasured his friendship, as he did theirs. As a WWII veteran, he was considered a national treasure, someone to be revered, and it was evident, in the way others addressed and treated him, that indeed he was. There were many genuine reasons for people to love and admire my dad. He was an engaging conversationalist with a brilliant mind—a compelling storyteller with a vast repertoire of interesting topics and unique personal experiences. One never needed to worry about pauses in conversation when Dad was in the room. Whether the listener was a stranger or an adoring grandchild, my father captured their undivided attention. They hung on his every word and were always left wanting to hear more—his listeners were enthralled by his narratives.

Dad was an educator with a lifelong thirst for learning and an unlimited capacity to retain information. He was also motivated to share his knowledge with anyone who listened, and he conveyed what he knew by storytelling. Hence, people understood and remembered what he said and ironically, they would learn without

1

realizing he was instructing them. Dad could combine words that stirred imaginations and brought any given topic to life leaving lasting impressions on his captivated audiences—not only with the spoken word. As you will discover in this book, he also loved to write—and did so articulately, and in great detail.

He was a multi-talented and accomplished artist and potter who painted an extensive gallery of artistic expressions depicting his life experiences. He literally memorialized his unique life story in beautiful art. Using his God-given talent to draw and his passion to create something of visual beauty, my father recorded his journey through life in brush strokes and colourful paint, giving credence to the expression, *a picture is worth a thousand words.*

It has been more than four years since my father died.

How can it simultaneously feel like yesterday, yet seem a thousand years ago? Perhaps it is just the way life is. One can feel sad but joyful, be old but youthful, so why should time be exempt from life's odd contrariness? On the day of Dad's memorial service, time itself seemed to stand still while my emotions raced out of control. I was overcome when conflicting feelings collided. I was happy, sad, stressed, and joyful—all at once! *How can that be, you wonder?* Let me explain.

I adored my dad, and I missed him with all my heart. The stories people shared were overwhelmingly lovely. They touched my soul and re-introduced me to my dad from *their* perspective. They affirmed all the characteristics I already knew, admired, and respected about Dad. He was everything they said and more. It was the *more* part that gripped me the most. When death stripped away all else, the only thing that mattered to me was who he was, and how much he meant to me.

I stood there inwardly battling emotions while I attempted to appear composed. I put on a brave front. After all, we were gathered to celebrate the life of my dad. The day was not about me or my loss. Nevertheless, the prevailing thought racing through my mind was loud and clear, and the words repetitive. I noted the underlying tone rang of defiance, which was an uncharacteristic behaviour for me, so I was also annoyed and bewildered. I wanted to yell out what I was thinking but due to decorum and respect I kept it to myself.

2

To me, he is just my dad.

I was thrilled that so many attended to pay their respects and to support our family, yet I was sad to bid farewell to him. This defining moment signalled the end of an era. I was joyful for him to be in heaven with my mother, yet the stress of what lay ahead (settling his estate) weighed me down. Hearing all the beautiful stories of the lives my dad touched made my soul sing for joy, but a gut-wrenching sadness gripped me deep within.

The loss hit home hard. There would be no more stories. No more paintings. No more belly laughs. That quirky grin—gone! No more morning and afternoon cups of tea with him. In his one last breath, all of who he was to me was snatched away. All except the memories—and my love for him. A random thought popped into my mind that reminded me of this captivating proverb.

When an old man dies, a library burns to the ground.
—African Proverb

As time passed and I published my own non-fiction book, I no longer focused so strongly on the *loss* of my dad. Instead, a fountain of gratitude sprung forth inside me that produced a rush of enthusiasm to assemble Dad's manuscripts and publish his memoirs. Over the years, I had often encouraged him to do so, but he would just flash me a knowing smile and softly remind me he had already written the stories and had provided his three grandchildren and me with copies. Touché Dad!

Despite the African Proverb and its inference about the loss of experience and wisdom when someone dies, perhaps I can at least resurrect *one* book from the ashes of the proverbial library. It is true that Dad's knowledge, wisdom, and talent left with his physical departure, yet so much of his essence remains—entrusted to me for safe keeping. My father left stories with me that tell of bygone days, and he wrote detailed accounts that uphold historical facts about WWII, all brought to life in his own articulate words describing those years. But that is not all—he also left paintings that speak louder than words.

This book contains stories written by my father—I have not changed his words—with accompanying chapters written by me, to provide further explanation, a back story, or a more in-depth glimpse into the man who was my dad. Let me add that his first story was from his childhood, while all the others relate to his experiences in WWII.

I feel sure many of you relate to what I have shared here. Our loved ones each carry with them meaningful stories that deserve to be remembered, and retold.

BOYS WILL BE BOYS
(Anthea)

Indeed! Even choirboys.

Do not be misled by those sweet voices lifted high to heaven, nor by the angelic countenance of the young lads in a church boys' choir, singing melodiously like songbirds. Choirboys are first and foremost boys—remember what they are made of—snips and snails and puppy dog tails, as the poem goes. At the very least boys are mischievous pranksters, bold risktakers who will challenge boundaries, and one might add they possess a smidgeon of daredevil. They are seemingly endowed with a natural streak of courage and quenchless thirst for adventure, exploration, testing authority and bucking the system.

The first of my father's stories has nothing to do with wartime really—yet you will discover it does—for it provides us with excellent insight into the nature of some of the boys who matured into valiant young men destined to fight for Great Britain in WWII. Some who returned changed forever, some who sadly never made it home. These men would have been grateful for their courage, their remarkable boldness, their belief in justice, and the undeniable compulsion to do their part for God, country—and the world. During wartime, they would have been especially thankful for camaraderie, and an unshakable foundation of faith in God.

As you read "The Choirboys" account, I hope you feel the boys' exuberance and camaraderie and catch their belief in fairness. Maybe their mischievous pranks will put a smile on your face as you recall *your* childhood days. Perhaps you will understand the boys' desire for fun, to rock the boat a little, to test the will and integrity of their superiors, and their willingness to challenge authority. Maybe you'll admire their stance for justice.

As you advance through this book and digest my father's wartime experiences, as seen through his eyes and written in his formal style of English, I am certain you (and especially those readers who knew him) will discover that many of the same characteristics he displayed as a mischievous choirboy remained

5

consistent in wartime, and indeed throughout his life. My dad's adventurous spirit, fair-mindedness, and his decisive, well thought out actions during his WWII service in the Fleet Air Arm branch of the Royal Navy, are some of the traits reflected in his memoirs.

The Choirboys: an original lino-cutting by J.A. Shipperlee, printed on Christmas cards

THE CHOIRBOYS OF ST. ANDREW'S C.E. CHURCH, LINTON ROAD, OXFORD.

(Tony)

The choir was not large, consisting of about eight boys and usually four to six men of whom three came to each practice and Sunday service while the others were frequent or only intermittent attenders.

John Lloyd was the 'head boy' or senior chorister. He was a few months older than most of us and was endowed with brains for he had been one of the only two eleven-year-old boys from all the Oxford elementary schools to be awarded a scholarship to Magdalen College School in his year. This scholarship was virtually an open competition, part of the 'eleven-plus' exam taken by every schoolboy in the city system between the ages of 10 ½ to 11 ½. He could sight-read music well, or certainly well enough for the purpose of most choirboys, and he knew how to use his voice to maximum effect. His voice was not an outstanding one, nor particularly sweet but reasonably strong and carried well around the church. John led the boys' section and held it together. He was not always the one selected to sing a solo part but could be relied upon to do so competently whenever needed, and thus he was asked to do so more often than any other boy.

John's brother 'Mick,' about 15 months younger, was also in the choir. He had not achieved the academic heights nor the singing efficiency of the elder Lloyd but played a useful supporting role and was constant in attendance.

'Pop' Trollope, aged 11 years, spoke of a 72-year-old father, and of being a son of his father's third wife. Geoffrey was his name, but he was invariably called 'Pop' due to his looks. He had a shock of tight curly hair of medium to light tone, and this, together with an abundance of wrinkles on the face, gave him the abnormal appearance for his age—that resulted in the nickname. One of several much older brothers had similar looks. These two boys, and I think other older brothers, went to the Municipal Secondary School, no doubt as scholars as they were bright. Later, the

7

Municipal Secondary school amalgamated with my selective secondary school and re-opened in 1934 as the newly built and well-endowed grammar school, "Southfield," which 'Pop' and I attended simultaneously for three years. As a chorister, Geoffrey was efficient and, possessing a comparatively sweet voice, was a useful member of the group.

We were to meet again much later in our careers.

During World War Two, 'Pop' had been a photographer in the Royal Air Force and towards the end of the war had been in a team, interpreting views taken by aerial reconnaissance planes. On demobilization, Trollope had been admitted to Oxford University to read geology. He became a good geologist, as would be expected with his intelligence and keenness for the subject. Pop soon began applying the knowledge and skills developed in the R.A.F., photographing terrain from two directions. He was able, by intuition or clever methods of his own, to deduce frequently correctly where oil and other highly valued products of the earth were likely to be lying. His successes reached the ears of people in South Africa like de Beers and Oppenheimer, and 'Pop' was sought after to forecast likely beds of such treasures, I understand, such as diamonds, gold, as well as oil.

Around 1961, during the three years I was Headmaster of the European School at Jinja, East Africa, 'Pop' Trollope and his wife called on Phyllis and me and had lunch with us in our home, before driving their land-rover-type vehicle towards the Congo. The Southfield 'Old Boys Association' had given him our address.

Several years later, probably in 1968, we received a telephone call in Beecroft, a suburb of Sydney Australia, from 'Pop' who was staying at a hotel in the city. We invited him to a meal that evening. However, he insisted that we met him in Sydney to be taken to dinner as he still had facts to record and recommendations to write before he departed from Australia the next day. Apparently, he had been on a speculative, exploratory trip to South America, Tasmania, and Western Australia, at the request and expense of one of the South African magnates and given

8

generous spending money. Phyllis and I rearranged our plan for the evening. We all enjoyed the brief re-union and a meal in the revolving restaurant overlooking the lights of Sydney and the harbour at the top of the recently completed 50-storey Australia Square tower. At the time of writing, we have heard of 'Pop' only rarely through contacts with 'old Southfieldians.'

Ken Hampson's future was less fortunate. He was a small lad, about a year younger than most of us. He joined several months after me and then travelled on the same bus as he lived only walking distance from me. Tragically, he was killed while flying in the R.A.F. in WWII, leaving parents forever grieving the loss of their only child.

Anthony (Tony) Long was another intelligent, academic boy. He attended the rival grammar school, the City of Oxford School, as did his elder brother, who had been in the choir in earlier years. Tony's voice was sweet and soft, and he was occasionally asked to sing a solo.

'Read', whose first name escapes me at present, also attended the City of Oxford School, paid for by his parents who were in better financial circumstances than the majority of the boys' parents as Mr. Read was a chain store managing-director. Mr. Read sometimes sang in the choir. The lad was a pleasant character who tended to join the stream rather than direct the currents. He was a steady, regular attender who helped to swell the numbers without making a significant difference to the quality of volume of the singing.

There must have been one or two others who overlapped part of my time in the choir, or possibly the whole of it—if so, I cannot remember them as they made no noteworthy mark by their presence.

Then there was 'Jimmy.' James Rolfe, the organist, and choirmaster was undoubtedly talented musically. Approaching middle age, Mr. Rolfe still lived with his mother—and apparently for her and his music. I can still clearly picture him sitting at the organ, leaning his body forward and back with frequent movements of the head. To us boys, he seemed rather detached, a little strange, and an eccentric. He invariably carried a large

9

black umbrella, wore spats, and with each step, he sprung off the ground as though springs were in the heels of his shoes. I recollect him wearing a bowler hat at times.

Jimmy's discipline was not effective. Perhaps because of still being resident with his elderly mother, unmarried without children, he did not seem to have a natural grasp of the techniques of handling boys at the age in which pranks were a common temptation. Or perhaps it was just the way Jimmy would have been anyway. Certainly, his uneasy manner and erratic approach to the situation fostered a frequent urge on the part of the choristers to indulge in a 'rag' of some sort—and his jumpy, unsound responses almost always amplified his troubles. No doubt as middle-aged citizens, we boys would have regarded Mr. Rolfe as a well-meaning, peace-loving able musician, but from the point of view of choristers aged around twelve, he was considered as just 'odd' enough to be fair game for larks. Adults seemed to respect his dedication, and he had gained some award when younger that had enabled him to attain a musical qualification—I think at Oxford University, for he wore a specialist's hood with his gown. The boys' practice started half-an-hour before the full choir practice, and that, of course, was the problem period for Jimmy.

There was the occasion when he was locked in the changing room—the room attached to the balcony area consisting of the organ and choir stalls. Jimmy's fuming and demanding to be let out provided great amusement for the boys. Doubtless, he later resorted to his usual retaliation of docking some of the choristers' pocket-money. The pay was intended to create competition and keenness among the youngsters. About three times a year, Jimmy conducted a contest in which each lad sang a short solo and tried to read a little musical score. They chanted several verses of a psalm (endeavouring to split and time all the words and phrases correctly) while attempting to keep in tune with and without the organ playing. Jimmy scored marks for various aspects in a system of his own. The higher up the list one finished, the higher the pay.

John Lloyd regularly came out at the top (due to his superior sight-reading skill and his confidence) as he deserved and thus received the one-and-sixpence per week—in those days, the cost of an excellent cinema seat or several bars of chocolate. Early in my membership, I once attained second place, which brought me one-shilling-and-threepence per week, but thereafter I hovered around the middle placings rated at one shilling. Some lads rarely proceeded beyond ninepence per week. Nobody appeared to be unduly jealous of anyone else, and I do not recall any boy grudging John Lloyd his permanent place at the top, for all fair-minded lads could see that he was rightly the 'top dog.'

The imprisonment of Jimmy would not have been of long duration for the expected arrival of the men would have signalled the turning of the key beforehand. This incident was probably one of the occasions when we all filtered around the church gardens and made ourselves inconspicuous behind bushes until the men began arriving. The crafty youngsters understood Jimmy would not then make a scene or, in some way, reveal to the other adults that he could not control the choristers. It was not the only time that half or more of the choir were hidden by the bushes causing Jimmy to go hunting around the grounds to the amusement of the boys.

Not rare, though not frequent, was the easing of songbooks to the edge of the balcony wall until they tipped over and fell to the nave floor. This activity was typically confined to practice periods, but I believe it took place once or twice when a function was in progress. In the latter instance, it would be due to carelessness or to some choirboy showing off by demonstrating how precariously he could position his books then misjudging the situation. Apart from creating a disturbing thud or report, the sudden sound would momentarily startle Jimmy, sometimes causing him to fumble a note. Not more than one low pile of books could be pushed over during a lengthy period, or the excuse of negligence or a mistake would not have any chance of being believed. There was one occasion when several books were slid over the edge, successively in a group 'plot' during the boys-only practice. The docking of pay usually followed, in theory, to help compensate for wear and tear on books.

Another, probably obvious, prank took place by a pre-arranged signal. At the start of a musical passage, no boy would produce a note. Jimmy would play the introductory bars, and at the intended moment of entry, no treble voice would be heard. He would remonstrate and begin again, but the non-performance would be repeated. Jimmy, with his face becoming redder and angry looking, would rave at us. At the third attempt, half the boys would sing, bringing Jimmy's wrath and threats upon those who did not. Thus, as the 'start' was reaching for the fourth time, the previous non-singers would begin while the other half would not. Normally, this not uncommon incident would last only a few minutes.

One evening we all felt that Jimmy had treated us unjustly. Before the commencement of singing with the men as a complete choir, there was a brief interval, sometimes used to 'dole out' the pocket money. Each boy was paid only a proportion of the amount he was expecting. Jimmy had fallen behind with payments, increasing the number of weeks between them but handing out only usual sums. For some obscure reason, he decided this was an opportunity to provide the youngsters with coins well below the value they believed was due to them.

As the lads gathered outside, their general annoyance grew into a combined determination to set things right. While an argument ensued between the organist and his choirboys, some lad brought up the view that might be taken by the churchwardens, which led to suggestions of complaining to one or other. When Jimmy ruffled the group still further, we met outside again and generally agreed we were not bluffing. While the youngest lad was despatched to inform Jimmy where we had gone, the rest marched off towards the nearest church warden's house—only one street distant. I recollect faintly the spectre of J.J.R. exerting himself on his bouncing gait rounding a corner in hot pursuit, and the need for us to break into a trot. Certainly, we reached the house first—then what? Decisions had to be made instantly, so I and another (probably Tony Long or the Read chap, though I cannot be sure now) volunteered to knock on the door while others held James at bay. I do recall clearly banging on the front door and starting the conversation going with a middle-aged, or slightly older, churchwarden, and the voices of other choristers soon joining in from the front path before the arrival of Jimmy perplexed the already dumbfounded warden still more. As any normal adult would react, he attempted to calm the troubled waters and promised to investigate it without indicating any criticism of the organist, and quite rightly.

The churchwarden played his cards well enough to enable the boys to return to the church, feeling that they had made a point and stood some chance of obtaining justice. The organist hurried back to the keyboard for the men had already gathered in the choirstalls. Some raised eyebrows were turned towards the boys as we trooped into our places. Rumours floated around that evening and the next Sunday.

I think the adults of the choir and a few others became aware of the revolt, but assumed it was a combination of irksome, but naturally high-spirited youngsters and a gifted but erratic temperament controlling them—or not controlling them. It all blew over very quickly. I seem to remember the lost pay was paid or partly paid. Somehow the affair evaporated without anyone losing too much face. By the time an intervening week had elapsed, the routine had returned to normal.

Similar attempts to rattle Jimmy would be made in other, less serious fashions now and again. I want to include some more positive aspects, however, as there were numerous occasions when we all pulled together, each giving of his best.

One involvement that remains in my memory was the participation of our choristers in an evening of short plays given by several small organizations—I think all choirs. A friendly competition was held, in full dress, in a hall in New Inn Hall Street, and was well supported by a large and appreciative audience. Jimmy and a friend had selected part of "The Wind in the Willows" for us to dramatize. Someone was 'Toad' who was being taken to court for a driving offence and others were 'Water-rat,' 'Badger,' etc. I was given the part of the judge and was so transformed by the adult who was making-up the faces that my relatives did not recognize me and were convinced I'd been replaced until they saw me after the performance. Everyone in the choir thoroughly enjoyed that evening.

Sometimes there were special services in other churches when we joined the choir of the host church, and on rare occasions, about three choirs would combine. On such afternoons or evenings, our choir would wear the surplices and cassocks of the colour worn by the boys of the 'home' choristers. We would leave off our traditional gear comprised of a black tie with high, stiff, white-collar (known as the Eton collar), a black gown, not full length but longer than the Oxford 'scholars' gown; and a mortar-board when outdoors.

Jimmy was fond of Bach's music, and it seemed to us that he played it very well—with sensitivity. Bach's choral works often featured in our singing, inevitably "Jesu, Joy of Man's Desiring." Other pieces I recall were "God Be in My Head" by Walford Davies, "Sheep May Safely Graze," and works by Stanford, including frequently the "Magnificat" and "Nunc Dimittis." The surroundings, atmosphere, being part of a choral group, and the music itself all helped to foster my early enjoyment in singing, and an appreciation of vocal music well performed.

FROM FINANCE TO FIERY BLITZ
(Anthea)

After graduating from Southfield School, a boy's secondary school in Oxford at that time, my father was employed in the accounting department of an education finance office. The war between Germany and Britain was already in full swing, and like so many other young men in Great Britain he was eager to serve his country, but much to his disappointment he was too young to join the military initially but when his turn did come, he was more than ready and willing to report for duty on February 3, 1941.

My dad was drafted into the Fleet Air Arm division of the Royal Navy. Here he is pictured soon afterwards.

Wars are brutal and devasting. They change everything, forever! The next story is the first of my father's wartime memoirs. This one as a 20-year-old newbie during his naval training. You might imagine the stark contrast he felt between the boring but comfortable finance office environment and bombs dropping all around during the Portsmouth bombardment—from finance to fiery blitz.

I am so very thankful that my father survived WWII and took the time to write down some of his various experiences from that era. Also, I am eternally grateful that he and so many others served and gave their utmost, alongside many allied forces, to crush the advancement of evil and oppression that threatened the world during the dark days of WWII.

The Blitz in Britain: According to "History.com", it has been estimated that during the eight months Blitz in Britain from September 1940 thru May 1941, about 40,000 civilians were killed,

46,000 injured, and more than a million homes destroyed and damaged in Britain, during this period. The word Blitz is a shortening of the German word blitzkrieg, meaning "lightning war," the literal translation of the German word "Blitz" is "lightning".

The Portsmouth Blitz: The City of Portsmouth, home to the Royal Navy, with facilities such as, Portsmouth Dockyard, and countless other military and industrial installations, was obviously a prime target for bombing raids by the German Luftwaffe. Portsmouth officially suffered 67 air raids between July 1940 and May 1944, three of these categorised as major attacks.

A NIGHT OF THE PORTSMOUTH BLITZ
(Tony)

Approximately two and a half weeks after my 20th birthday, I reported on 3rd February 1941 to H.M.S. St. Vincent in Gosport for the initial course in the Fleet Air Arm. This was for three months naval instruction from experienced petty officers, serving under a few officers. It included Morse code and semaphore, boat work, parade ground drill, sea navigation under Commander Spink, naval customs and terminology and various other types of training.

"St. Vincent" was a large and long-established shore base for instructing various ratings, aircraft radio operators, potential pilots, and observers, several hundred in all. My pilot's course numbered around 115. Gosport faced across the narrow entrance of the harbour to Portsmouth and thus received part of the bombing during the periods of "the Portsmouth Blitz".

During my service there, we were subjected to night raids two or three times each week. On such evenings, when not on duty, we all had to sleep in underground cellars. Trainees were divided into four groups: 1st and 2nd Port Watches (red) and 1st and 2nd Starboard Watches (green). The Port Watches were on duty one night, the Starboard Watches the next. There were two types of duty, so we each performed two nights in four, alternating between the "pick and shovel party" and the "station fire engine squad". The latter consisted of three or four mobile fire pumps manned by six or eight of us per machine and hauled by us to the spot needed.

The pick and shovel party had to tramp some three-quarters of a mile to an oil dump comprised of several large circular oil storage tanks which rose 25 or 30 feet from the ground and could be ascended by a fixed metal ladder. Our task was to disperse among these storage tanks and watch for incendiary bombs, climbing the ladders to throw dirt on any firebombs that landed on top of the oil containers. Rain often made the surrounding ground mucky, so the 'pick and shovel party' had become commonly called 'the ---- and shovel party'—with a vulgar four-letter word replacing the first one.

There was a particularly heavy raid one evening when my group were manning a fire pump. We could hear the anti-aircraft guns firing high into the sky and see flashes from various directions caused by bombs. Also, a mighty roar would occasionally rumble from the harbour—made by the 12-inch guns of an obsolete French battleship of World War One that had joined the Free French Forces in Britain after the fall of France the previous June. These guns in turrets could be angled high and shells were fired blindly into the sky in the direction of the bombers. They probably never hit an enemy plane but falling shrapnel may have caused damage somewhere—the main effect being psychological, to add to the sound of the retaliatory fire from the ground, and to boost the morale of the French sailors brooding over their inaction in an allied but foreign port.

Our mobile pump was based in a garage in the corner of a rear quadrangle, and we wheeled this around to extinguish incendiaries landing in our sector. Soon there was a need to rush to the NAAFI canteen which had been ignited and the flames were rapidly spreading among the stores of cigarettes, tobacco, cakes, and sweets, etc. We faced a blaze and aimed a powerful jet of water onto it. Before many minutes, the fire was under control. About the time it was nearly extinguished there came the sound of a high explosive bomb hitting the ground some distance behind us and to our right. This was quickly followed by a second, then a third, each getting closer in our direction.

We immediately dived for cover! I lay on the ground against the bottom of a high wall that had been behind me, hoping that any more bombs in the 'stick' (of probably six) would land far enough on the other side of the wall for it to give shelter. There was a fourth high explosive burst closer still—and then a fifth.

I distinctly recall thoughts flashing through my mind of the problems experienced in the finance office before joining the navy and telling myself how petty they all seemed now, and vowing that if I survived the war, I would subdue worries over all such comparatively trivial matters! Meanwhile I estimated that a sixth would explode remarkably close to the wall and I anticipated its arrival in a state of great tension, for several seconds—and more seconds—but it did not come. Perhaps one bomb had failed to go off, so I waited for a late detonation.

When that did not occur in the next few moments, I picked myself up to join my comrades in gathering once more around the mobile pump. Finishing off the remnants of the canteen fire, we began moving the engine towards its base but as we did so, another two or three high explosive bombs burst at a safe distance from ourselves but in the vicinity of the oil

18

depot. One crashed through the metal top of a tank as it exploded, sending a great flash of light into the dark night and, as this diminished, a yellowish flame lit the sky from the burning oil flung upwards by the blast, and the oil remaining ignited within the tank.

Almost immediately we became aware of numerous small spots of light descending from above. They were drops of burning oil, which resembled raindrops dripping from the sky. Our squad hurriedly pushed and pulled the fire pump to the garage and took shelter from this peculiar phenomenon, meanwhile flicking off those isolated blobs that settled on our outer overalls supplied for this fire duty. Thankfully, our heads were protected by tin helmets.

With the garage door open, observing the continuing fall of scattered drips of burning oil, I reflected upon the good fortune of there being only five bombs in the high explosive stick that had descended towards my group. I wondered if two could have burst simultaneously, or if I could have miscounted during the haste to lie at the base of the wall, or if five was the number intended for that batch. The answer I knew was unlikely ever to be revealed unless a line of holes next day gave a clue, but these would be in awkward places to check, and anyway I would be otherwise occupied.

Already my thoughts were turning to the 2nd Port squad and a sinking feeling came upon me concerning those course mates whose turn it had been to do duty in the storage depot. My close friend Grahame had been in that group, and I felt sickly at the idea of him or one of the others atop the container that had received the direct hit.

Hours passed as we pondered awful possibilities and snatched what periods of sleep were possible on types of sleeping bags on the concrete floor.

Luckily, the raid had passed over without further bombing in our area. It was still an hour or two before we were able to meet the returning 'pick and shovel party' and learn with considerable relief that no-one had been on the tank that had been ripped open by the high explosive, and despite unpleasant and dangerous experiences the party had not sustained casualties.

Having been witness to hours of blitz these facts seemed miraculous. On other nights more raids occurred but I recall that one as the worst that I remember of the Portsmouth Harbour period of training.

FULL STEAM AHEAD
(Anthea)

It is with a great deal of nostalgia that I recall the bygone era of steam trains. There was something so romantic about a steam engine puffing away from a station platform, or clickety-clacking along the track through the English countryside, all the while billowing clouds of white and grey smoke high into the sky. I can confirm that my father *loved* steam trains. From the time he was a young boy his father would take him (and years later, me) on day excursions to nearby train stations—most likely Oxford, Reading, and Didcot to name a few—to spot for trains.

Trainspotting was the name of the game. Enthusiasts would record the engine numbers of the different trains in a book with hopes of collecting the identity of as many of the different trains and train lines as was possible. In those days, bicycles, buses, and trains were the most essential modes of transportation so my dad would have ridden his bicycle or taken a bus ride—or two or three—to the chosen train station.

My father developed such an avid interest in steam locomotives that he grew knowledgeable as to which engines travelled on specific railway lines. As a lad who loved trainspotting, he also enjoyed playing with toy windup trains—exact replicas of the real model and track. In his teenage years, during holidays he would ride his bicycle many miles from his hometown in Oxford to locations such as the Southwest counties—Dorset, Somerset, Devon, Cornwall and more—often following the roads that paralleled the train tracks.

I believe these experiences led to my dad's vast understanding and knowledge of trains, where their hubs were located, where the tracks started and ended, where they intersected other railway lines, and which towns and roads were close by. He even knew the departure times of certain main line trains. He became an expert at reading maps and thereby learning the lay of the land in relation to train tracks. This would all prove invaluable to him during the war, as you will discover in a few of the train stories in this book. The next two accounts demonstrate that train travel was not only a

21

method of transport but presented opportunities for unusual and unexpected experiences, as well as interesting encounters.

Trains featured prominently in my father's wartime experiences but long after steam locomotives were replaced by modern train technology and engineering, and automobiles became more affordable and obtainable, his passion for trains burned strong and bright. While that era has faded into history for most people today, the beauty of the steam engine lives on—memorialized in the artistic train paintings that my father lovingly and expertly painted in oils, forever glorifying their existence.

TRAIN STORIES – REMARKABLE COINCIDENCE
(Tony)

Soon after commencing the third stage of Fleet Air Arm pilot training at the aerodrome at Netheravon, my "watch" became due for a weekend leave, which came around every four weeks all being well. The aerodrome was on Salisbury Plain about 12 miles from the city. Further north were only small villages for a long distance. At that time, little traffic used the road, so it was imperative to catch the evening bus passing through the village, as it was probably the last of the day. It likely terminated at Marlborough for it was due to pass through Pewsey at 6:45 pm where there was a small station and a local stopping train five minutes later enroute for Reading.

If the train were missed the only hope was hitchhiking. On a major road that would not have been daunting as summer was only just ending "double summertime". I had hitchhiked very successfully to Oxford on several occasions from Portsmouth and Birmingham, distances of 77 and 64 miles respectively, but along the quiet Pewsey Road it would be quite a different matter. With severe petrol rationing cars were scarce, maybe one an hour, and the trucks, although more frequent on the Birmingham Road, were virtually non-existent here. I would most likely be stranded overnight. It was essential for that bus to reach Pewsey on time.

The bus was not prompt in getting to Netheravon, and then it moved along sluggishly, stopping at each hamlet. The few minutes gap between the scheduled bus arrival and the train departure were soon lost. It became obvious that it was touch and go if the connection would be made, and the driver cared not whether he reached places on time. One could be forgiven, surely, for silently cursing the driver and making remarks hinting at the need to reach Pewsey punctually. They fell on deaf ears. I learned that there were no arrangements between the bus company and the railway. My discovery from timetables that a train could be caught if the bus ran to time was merely coincidental.

As the bus finally stopped in Pewsey, I could see a short train at the far platform—clearly the one I needed. I hurried up the inclined approach road from the village to the station, about 100 yards. Lugging my suitcase, I began a quick trot for I could see the signal already down, indicating

23

"go". The train had to be reached by climbing a footbridge from the near platform leading over the tracks. My fears were realized when the engine emitted steam and its wheels started turning well before I had placed a foot on the first step of the bridge. By the time I was halfway across it, the last of the three carriages was beyond the platform and moving at a speed not likely to permit catching it.

"Drat it and damn that blasted bus driver," I thought, *"and the whole system that fails to tie up a proper connection with local trains, especially in times when private transport was at a premium."*

As such thoughts filled my head and I made my way disconsolately to the first platform I realized that my attempt to catch the train had not gone unnoticed. The porter-stationmaster sympathised but could only confirm that no more trains were due at Pewsey that night. We stood talking briefly while I contemplated what to do. On turning to leave the area I observed the approach of a second railway worker. He was the signal operator who had descended the steps from the signal building approximately eighty yards along the track. He informed his workmate that the train had contained one coachload of soldiers but an extra wagon full of their equipment had not been properly linked to the rear carriage and had been left behind. It was being hurried along the rails by a special locomotive to catch the company of troops at the next stopping place.

The two railwaymen conferred momentarily and then suggested that I should stand outside the signal box and the signalman would halt the "pursuit" locomotive. Moments later the engine and single wagon came into sight. As they stopped at the signal the railwayman and I quickly explained my predicament to the driver who jovially welcomed me aboard.

This was in 1941 when the threat of invasion was fresh in everyone's mind for Britain had stood alone against Hitler's war machine for a year until the German invasion of Russia only three months previously. The Japanese and USA had not yet entered the war. Most people (certain bus drivers excepted!) were very friendly and helpful to servicemen in uniform at that time, as shown in this example.

We caught up with the train carrying the army personnel after a few miles, when a relayed message delayed it in a little station so that the wagon could be coupled. At Reading, it was easy for me to obtain rail transport to Oxford, only 30 miles distant.

TRAIN STORIES - JUST ONE OTHER PASSENGER
(Tony)

When a very young, inexperienced, extremely new, and junior officer, I was proceeding from the Portsmouth area on a brief visit to Oxford bearing an official rail pass issued by the Navy. Reaching one of the local stations, I found the Basingstoke & London train already at the platform and ready to depart. So, I hurried to a 1st Class carriage (as entitled by the 1st class pass), opened the door of one of the six- seat compartments, pushed my case onto the floor and mounted the step into the compartment. Quickly I lifted the case up onto the rack and turned to sit in a spacious, comfortable seat beside a window.

It was then that I had a full view of the only other occupant. I had already been vaguely aware of his presence, though I'd not really observed him as my back had been towards him while lifting my case previously, and while clambering hastily into the carriage my eyes had been on the case and then on the rack.

He was a middle-aged to elderly naval officer, of stoutish but not plump build and moderate or medium height. He relaxed back into the corner seat opposite. With some surprise and a great deal of misgiving, I noticed on his sleeves the broad gold band below three normal bands – a full Admiral. The rapidly growing feeling of uneasiness prompted me to begin mumbling something in the nature of a question as to whether the compartment was reserved or if it were all right to sit there, but the Admiral was already intent on putting me at ease by smiling and asking if I were going on leave and where was my destination.

For a while he chatted pleasantly in a fatherly manner, and I left that train with the distinct feeling that there was a most human and gentlemanly person, perhaps also possessing a kindly sense of humour. Later, on enquiring among more knowledgeable people, I learned that he was almost certainly Sir William James, Commander-in-Chief of the Portsmouth Division of the Home Fleet.

I wish I could meet that benevolent man again now to let him read my thoughts on this brief incident.

A note of interest: Since writing this anecdote, my wife Phyllis and I stayed in Oxford in 1991 with a friend, Sydney Brookfield, who was a Lieut-Commander in the Admiralty in WWII, designing parts of artificial harbours; on reading this account of the meeting with Admiral James, he told us that the Admiral, in WWII was still known in the Admiralty as "Bubbles".

Bubbles was the little boy with blonde curly hair, who used to advertise Pears' soap, a well-known poster depicting the boy holding a bowl of soap-suds and blowing bubbles with a clay pipe. Apparently, the early photograph had earned the Admiral the name throughout his career.

By the way, the posters of "Bubbles" were from a portrait painted by the little boy's grandfather, Sir John Everett Millais, P.R.A., and exhibited at the Royal Academy. The painting was sold to The Illustrated London News, then later purchased by A & F Pears for two thousand guineas for use in their advertisement.

THE EXTRAORDINARY WALRUS
(Anthea)

Another mode of transportation would soon capture my father's attention, and his heart. These machines would feature prominently in his military life—planes. Flying machines, and during his Fleet Air Arm service, Tony flew fourteen different aircraft in missions and manoeuvres.

The following story involves a Walrus—not the ocean swimming, tusked variety, but rather the seafaring aircraft. I thought it appropriate to provide you with some background facts and a little light-hearted humour regards the flying Walrus. Of all the aircraft flown during WWII, the Supermarine Walrus seaplane would most likely top the list of my father's favourites. He often spoke with nostalgia about his wartime experiences in the Walrus, though I recall (as far back as a child of about 5 years old) hearing my father and his friends speaking facetiously about the seaplane, making the "old rust bucket" Supermarine Walrus the butt of some jokes—rightly or wrongly calling into question the construction of the machine.

The Walrus was described as the sturdiest aircraft ever built. It was designed to be catapulted from warships with a full military load and hoisted back on-board ship as it floated alongside after a water landing. It was quite a remarkable machine—it could land on a carrier, land on the water, taxi to the shore, use conventional runways, and be catapulted off a battleship or cruiser at 6Gs, and capable of performing an outside loop. It was affectionately known as the "Shagbat " or sometimes "Steam-pigeon"; the latter name coming from the steam produced by water striking the hot Pegasus engine.

According to military.wikia.org: "The Supermarine Walrus was a British single-engine amphibious biplane reconnaissance aircraft designed by R. J. Mitchell and first flown in 1933. It was operated by the Fleet Air Arm (FAA) and also served with the Royal Air Force (RAF), Royal Australian Air Force (RAAF), Royal Canadian Air Force (RCAF), Royal New Zealand Navy (RNZN) and Royal New Zealand Air Force (RNZAF). It was the first British squadron-service aircraft to incorporate a fully retractable main undercarriage,

27

completely enclosed crew accommodation, and an all-metal fuselage."

My father would enthusiastically recall his missions in the Walrus. It seems to me that Dad's time in this flying machine, while in the water and above land, resulted in him forming a deep respect and clear understanding of the intricacies of the seaplane. He knew its workings inside and out intimately—its shortcomings and strengths. Later in the war, he would share his knowledge with his younger protégés. One very important fact he emphasized as follows:

"A walrus can be more dangerous than a land plane," he would caution. "Remember, when landing an aircraft on land, the ground stays put whereas the sea does not. Not only can the sea be very wavy and choppy, but it can move in different directions. You can have the wind coming one way, and the sea going another way—so what do you do? Do you level against the wind, or against the swell of the sea, or halfway? You had to consider the wind, estimate its strength, factor in the size of the waves, and decide which is more important. Then you would adjust as needed this way or that way. However, there's one more thing to remember. When you land on the ground, you make sure the wheels are down. When you land on water the last thing you do is have your wheels down or they will dig into the water and turn the plane upside down. Every time that has happened, the pilot was killed. So, *never* ever have wheels down on a water landing." Great advice indeed!

It was not until I became an adult, that I fully understood the significance of the frequent fun my mother and father enjoyed at the expense of the Walrus. I would simply join in the merriment as they delivered a few lines from a poem. It was catchy and they recited it with great enthusiasm and raucous laughter. It was common for my dad (and through the years sometimes my mother who was in the WRNS in WWII, affectionately known as a Wren) to smilingly open a conversation, when timing seemed appropriate, with the lines from Lewis Carroll's famous poem "The Walrus and the Carpenter."

"The time has come" the Walrus said, "to talk of many things." But that's where Lewis Carroll's poetry ended, and the remaining lines morphed into a "knockoff" that described the Walrus aircraft, as follows:

"The time has come", the Walrus said,
"To talk of many things —
Of pusher-screws and Shagbats *
And strutted, swept-back wings.
I'm an aeronautical wonder
And if that is not enough,
Then I've wheels that I can land on
When the sea's a bit too rough."

E.A. Wren, after Lewis Carroll

"Shagbat" – a humourous, but undignified naval epithet bestowed on the feathered variety of seagull.

Refuelling a Walrus Aircraft

29

A LITTLE SHOPPING TRIP
(Tony)

At the beginning of 1943, an Admiralty signal instructed me to travel to the small Royal Naval Air Station at Broughty Ferry, Dundee, to R.N.A.S. Twatt in the Orkney Islands in readiness to join one of the warships of the Home Fleet based in Scapa Flow. A few fellow "Walrus" pilots had already gone from Broughty Ferry to the Headquarters Squadron, No. 700, awaiting allocation to a cruiser or larger warship, and several more would follow. Although the brief episode related below did not happen to me personally, it was grim reality for two of my fellow aviators, and of such rare occurrence to be recorded in my recollections of those times.

Approaching Christmas Day, they found a reason to call at the other R.N.A.S. at Hatston, meet comrades there for drinks, and accomplish a little shopping at the nearby small town of Kirkwall—by landing in a convenient bay close by. After alighting on the surface, they slowly taxied along the water seeking a mooring. Boats were tied to the jetty and buoys. Soon they located a suitable buoy without any craft attached. The observer went to the nose hatch position, leaned over, and firmly fastened the seaplane's line to the buoy.

"Make sure it's well secured," stressed his friend.

"It certainly is," replied the observer.

They scanned the beach and jetty and hailed a fisherman in a small boat who rowed to the aircraft and then the short distance to the jetty. The aircrew tipped the elderly boatman and enquired if he would be around in two or three hours.

"I usually am, or one of my mates is here," they were told.

So off they strode, spending time in Kirkwall and at the R.N.A.S. Hatston, probably being given lifts by their friends. In due course, they returned to the edge of the small bay, where again they were welcomed aboard a rowboat. But they could not see the aeroplane. The oarsman took them to the spot where it had been moored, and they felt quite certain they had returned to the exact position; unfortunately, the buoy was not there either, nor was it in sight. After rowing around and searching the locality for several minutes it became clear that both aircraft and buoy were missing. Could they have sunk or been stolen? Or perhaps other aircrews had played a prank on them. One of the men set off for the R.N.A.S. to make enquiries and subsequently returned with companions bearing field glasses.

The searchers carried out a steady gaze through binoculars, around the shoreline, and across the water to more distant islands. Before long, a suspicious speck four or five miles distant was revealed. It was a Walrus aircraft stranded on a gently shelving beach.

Embarrassing explanations ensued with the usual enquiry by more senior staff of the parent ship, but I did not hear of any drastic consequences. It was fortunate that currents had swept the plane onto comparatively soft material without rocks where it became grounded. Inspection showed that the Walrus was virtually undamaged, and it was soon re-floated, and flown to base for servicing. The buoy had been still attached to the aircraft when located.

Unfortunately, the aircrew had moored to a loose, floating buoy that had just happened to be in the bay at the time.

HURRICANE IN THE ARCTIC
(Anthea)

It was December 1958, and our family was on board a ship bound for East Africa, where Dad had accepted a three-year tour as Headmaster of a primary school in Jinja, Uganda. We found ourselves in the Bay of Biscay, an area renowned for its high seas and storms in the wintertime. The previous evening, as a lark, my father had participated in a fancy-dress event, causing quite a stir when his turn came to parade in front of our fellow passengers. You see, he decided to pose as Adolf Hitler. After combing his black hair to one side and painting on a fake mustache, his appearance bore a striking resemblance to Adolf Hitler, as he clicked his heels, raised his arm straight out, and shouted "Heil Hitler!" I think Dad was unprepared for the response. Many people were startled and somewhat fearful—after all it was only 13 years since the end of WWII and events would still be fresh in the minds of some. Several people approached him later for reassurance that he was only an imposter. Thankfully, Dad's "lark" was amiably received by most, but it does further illustrate the bravado my father possessed—a boldness and quirky humour that emerged at various times in his life.

The next day was Christmas Eve and the ship's dining room was virtually deserted. I was feeling a little nauseated with no appetite. My dad, who was rather white-faced himself, exclaimed "The last time I experienced this kind of rolling and tossing at sea was during a wartime expedition in the Arctic, on board H.M.S. Sheffield, before you were born. Mind you Anthea, that was a much fiercer storm!" Shortly after his comment, both Dad and I staggered from the dining room in search of the nearest restrooms. Amazingly, my mother was fine, although concerned for us.

The sea sickness lasted for almost three days but finally we adjusted to the tossing and lurching of the vessel. It was then that Dad provided me with a summary of his next story—which is a more detailed account of his encounter with the severe Arctic hurricane in 1943.

Many years after the wartime hurricane, in 2014, while visiting my parents in the quiet town of Sturminster Newton, where they

32

resided, I had the honor to witness the arrival of a small package, addressed to my father. Inside was a special and meaningful award that delighted Dad—one that he obviously valued. It was the Arctic Star.

The Arctic Star is a retrospective award to those who served on the Arctic Convoys during the Second World War, of which my father was one. It was formally approved by Queen Elizabeth II, nearly seventy years after the end of WWII.

My father's account that follows, called *Northern Seas*, details events at sea amidst a devastating hurricane while he was assigned to H.M.S. Sheffield on an Arctic Convoy. The storm had been recorded in the Admiralty as the fiercest in which a ship of the Royal Navy had been involved.

NORTHERN SEAS
(Tony)

Late in February 1943, H.M.S. Sheffield, a medium cruiser of 10,000 tons, sailed from Scapa Flow to shadow and provide cover for Convoy JW53 of 28 merchant ships bound for Murmansk on the Arctic Coast of Russia. This route led via the North Sea into the Arctic Circle and the Barents Sea, notorious for wild weather, furious seas, and freezing temperatures. Now the perils of nature were joined by additional hazards—the U–boat menace and raids by German aircraft based in Scandinavia. At this time of year, it was imperative to keep further away from the Pole than was possible in summer, to avoid the icesheets. This brought vessels in winter closer to the U-boat and aircraft bases in Northern Norway. Winter conditions could also handicap the enemy with long hours of darkness (almost continuous at times), poor day-light visibility due to mists and fogs, and the biting cold.

I had been sent to the Orkney Island F.A. A. Base at Twatt early in January to team up with my observer and air-gunner and work as the crew of Walrus Z1761 and join H.M.S. Sheffield. This was our first voyage together and my very first real ocean voyage. The observer was Christopher Stubbs, then scarcely twenty-one and rather more than a year younger than me. His parents (a doctor and a nurse) had moved to New Zealand when Christopher was an infant and he had grown up on the coast of South Island; so, he had made a lengthy sea voyage within the past year, for training in Britain with the Fleet Air Arm. We and the air-gunner were the only three flying members of the crew of approximately 600. There were half-a-dozen or so maintenance crew to work on the engine, rigging, gun, etc. Originally the ship had two aircraft and crews, but these had been lost in a tragic accident when they flew into each other. After that, the ship's commander (2nd-in-command) had persuaded Captain Addis to ask for only one aircraft and crew as one of the smaller hangers had become too useful as a potato and general store, while the other had long been used for giving group instruction and cinema shows for crews in harbour. Before sailing, therefore, we had been craned aboard from the waters of Scapa Flow and hoisted on to the catapult, the device running across the ship amidships for launching the aircraft directly over the side.

The Sheffield had four turrets, each with three 6-inch guns (firing shells of 6 inches in diameter). The vessel had been on this type of convoy duty a few times previously, and usually met two or three cruisers of similar size, and several destroyers at some point along the route, to provide stronger protection from the heavy German cruisers and one or two pocket-battleships that were known to be lurking in the Norwegian harbours much of the war. They would venture out to attack the convoys to Murmansk from time to time and aid the U-boats and aircraft in sinking tens of thousands of tons of shipping and supplies.

On this occasion H.M.S. Sheffield was making most of the voyage alone, expecting to be in the proximity of the convoy only during its period of greatest danger. From the start the winds were strong and the seas rough. During the second day they became fierce, and by the time the ship was somewhere N.E. of Iceland, inside the Arctic Circle, the weather condition had become cyclone. Winds of over 100 knots had whipped up the surface of the water into a continuous grey mass—a horizontal sheet of spray that extended above the ship and made it impossible to distinguish between the sky and the sea. It all looked the same—grey, wet, and flying past at great speed.

Only through small openings of thickly glassed portholes could any looks be sneaked. No-one was allowed on deck, for to venture there would have been certain suicide. For about two days the warship remained facing the wind, engines turning just enough to maintain a mere 2 1/2 knots—sufficient to keep the bows pointing in the desired direction. The violent waters pounded the vessel causing it to pitch and roll severely, while creaks and groans in the structure and movements in the expansion plates were at times all quite alarming. I was extremely glad to be aboard a British ship built at Newcastle-upon-Tyne only a few years previously.

Being quite unaccustomed to such large and continuous heaving and twisting motions, I was frequently seasick—about hourly for a day and a half. Twenty-four hours of that time I could only lie in my bunk feeling very bilious, miserable, and apprehensive. Christopher, amazingly, seemed almost normal and was able to attend the wardroom at mealtimes to partake of any food that a stalwart cook had been able to provide.

He reported that few others joined him. Already his future successful bedside manner (as a family doctor in New Zealand) was showing and he came frequently to cheer me up, give advice and inform me how the ship was standing the strain. Apparently considerable quantities of water were getting inside certain parts of the cruiser. Enormous waves were beating against the armour-plating; many were crashing past the bows and breaking on the foredeck or against 'A' turret; one had crashed with such weight and force that it had buckled & opened the steel turret, causing injuries to the forward gun crew. One had a broken jaw & another a broken arm. Guns had been pointed sideways to minimize water running down the barrels, as the end-disks had not been screwed on beforehand in case of action stations being sounded. There was little likelihood of any hostility by this time for any other vessel (or aircraft) in the vicinity would be fully occupied in surviving the hurricane-force gale, and no submarine could contemplate nearing the surface to fire a torpedo in such wild conditions.

Around the third day the cyclonic winds eased and after a while it became possible to see on deck the havoc caused by the frightening storm. No small boat or lifeboat remained intact; stern and stem posts were still lashed in position but most of the middle of each boat was missing, leaving ragged assortments of planking hanging to their fasteners. The life-floats had virtually all been swept overboard. The submarine detection mechanism had been swept from under the hull, and the radar gear had been blown off the superstructure; 200 tons of seawater were estimated to be in the hull. The most forward turret was of course unlikely to work properly if needed. At some stage, a signal was sent to the Admiralty reporting the situation, but I do not know if it went off immediately or after the ship had limped to Iceland, due to radio silence. As the vapour cleared from above the ocean the enormity of the swell became clear. Mountainous walls of water rose above the horizon and surged towards the warship, dwarfing it as the cruiser was in the hollows, by towering over the superstructure, then crashing over the foredeck and subsequently lifting it up like a giant hand, to be carried upon the massive bank of sea before settling briefly again in the next trough. Officially the waves were recorded as being around 70 feet high; some looking a hundred feet higher at the crest than in the trough; they were certainly high and obscured all waves beyond them as well as the horizon. The sights were spectacular, the sensation unreal, as though riding the surface of a fluid range of low hills.

Although the tendency to seasickness slowly decreased it did not disappear and I was not able to eat. Many of the ship's company suffered from the motion sickness. Even "old sweats" who had spent all their working lives at sea and had been recalled for the duration of war, confessed to feeling the malady for the first time since their youth. I found myself wandering around the interior of the ship to divert my attention from the unpleasant sensation and snatching breaths of fresh air whenever a spot was reached with an opening to the breeze. As an aircrew we had things to attend to related to the aircraft in the normal way but now, of course, such activities as anti-submarine patrols were not appropriate. In such slack periods it would not be long before the executive commander found some duties for us. Meanwhile the ship headed for Seydhisfjordhur, the small, but second, town of Iceland on its east coast, nestled in the neck of the fjord of that name, and well sheltered from the ocean.

A few other vessels were anchored in the fjord; a sister ship of our cruiser, two or three merchant ships and several fishing boats. All were dwarfed by the immense walls of the fjord which rose straight from the sea at a steep angle, rugged, barren with marked horizontal strata and score marks sweeping down to the water, as though some giant hack-saw blade had scraped them. That evening it was a novelty to walk along the main street and see the lights on everywhere, spreading up the slopes of the rocky terrain, for the blackout in Britain had obliterated such sights for over three years. The friendly little lights gave the place an air of fairyland. It was an exceedingly small town by European standards, not much more than a large village, but the equivalent of a local pub enabled us to taste the Danish beer and exchange friendly nods with the inhabitants. How good it was to walk on firm ground.

Next morning Captain Addis decided that the aircraft should be test-flown as he or the Commander might need to visit an Icelandic Government representative or an Allied regional representative ashore, and in any case when the cruiser put to sea again an anti-submarine patrol might be required.

37

The walrus had been turned into wind soon after H.M.S. Sheffield left Scapa Flow and all through the cyclone had been on the catapult between the funnels, exposed to the full fury of the wind and spray but clear of the beating waves. The maintenance crew checked it over and could find no obvious damage. So, Christopher and I put on flying clothes and climbed into the amphibian. We were joined by our air-gunner, Leading Airman Allison. In the Walrus we were lifted from the ship by a small crane and lowered onto the surface of the fjord, which, due to the splendid shelter from the high slopes on both sides, was ideal for a water take-off—rippling with small wavelets, but overall flat and calm. A still, mirror surface could be bad for judging height on the subsequent landing, and a rough swell would cause uncomfortable jolts for us, and shaking and buffeting for the aircraft, on both take-off and landing, so the fjord provided an excellent opportunity to test the amphibian in favourable conditions.

After taxiing around for a couple of minutes or so, checking the operation of throttle, engine, rudder, ailerons, etc., I turned the amphibian into wind and pushed the throttle well forward. As we sped along the face of the water leaving a 'V' of disturbed ripples and bubbles in our wake we could look for any sign of cracks or leaks. All seemed well and I accelerated to fast speed-boat pace without any warning sounds or jets of liquid squirting into the hull. Applying full throttle, I eased the plane onto its step near the centre of gravity of the hull, and we maintained a straight and steady track along the wavelets. Quickly the Walrus raised itself high in the sea and lifted clear of the water. Briefly I kept the plane just a few feet up to check that the engine would maintain power and increase height as required. The response to this was good. But at once it was necessary to press on one foot-pedal and hold the control column a bit to one side to maintain straight and level flight. This need remained, indicating that the aircraft had suffered some strain during the gale—it was a little warped! However, we were airborne over the fjord! Apart from the defect, Walrus Z1761 was flying, and its engine was not faltering. We soon were reassured that it was likely to maintain a safe condition. Though there had been misgivings before leaving the warship, and for the early minutes in the plane, we felt we could now claim that Z1761 had withstood the fury of the Arctic cyclone well enough to continue to be of service.

The Walrus was put through a few exercises, and we enjoyed the views of the Icelandic coast before gliding close to the "Sheffield" and alighting on the water, fifty minutes after taking off. Chugging in the sea, under/hook of a crane derrick, we fastened the hook to the special ring in the upper wing of the plane and switched off. It was either the air-gunner's or observer's task to clamber onto the wings and do the fixing, though pilots had practiced this job during our seaplane training. The crane then hoisted us aboard and rested the Walrus once more on the catapult. It later received some adjustment to the rigging and controls to minimize the effects of the twist sustained by the plane. This test flight occurred on 23rd February 1943.

The ship was ordered to return to the Clyde for repairs. There followed a pleasant voyage along the West coast of Scotland, through The Minch & past the Hebrides and the Mull of Kintyre. I say pleasant for we were away from the vicious Arctic area, in a region unlikely to suffer air attack, and not noted for U-boat activity. The sea was still heaving enough to cause moderate movement of the cruiser, but by spending much of my time on deck in fresh air I could keep my tendency to sickness under control, and even enjoy light, rather dry meals. Boosting all our spirits was the realization that not only were we heading for our home country, but we were almost certain to be granted two or three weeks leave while the ship was being repaired.

The "Sheffield" docked at Greenock. Three days after the test flight in Seydhisfjord, Christopher Stubbs and I were again aboard the Walrus, this time to be catapulted direct from the ship. This mechanism was made ready for launching, the aircraft was again serviced, our cases and personal gear were lashed securely in the hull. Then, with the engine and propeller at full speed, causing the aircraft to quiver violently while stationary, I lowered my arm from the vertical position to show the officer in-charge of the catapult that we were ready to be 'fired'. He lowered his arm to indicate that the cordite charge was being set up. A small jolt informed us that the detonator had fired—there was a momentary pause and then the aeroplane surged forward, rapidly gathering speed and the invisible hand that pressed into our backs flung us the final yards across the ship with such force that we blacked out for a split second (as was normal) and came round with the skin pressed back along the sides of our faces and the feeling of leaving stomachs back amidships. In that moment of revival, the Walrus left the ship's side at around 56 knots (approx. 65 mph.), sank a few feet while attaining its speed for full 'lift' and then began to gain height.

Rising above the shipping and small boats in the Clyde estuary we headed north-eastwards, obtaining a lovely panoramic view of Loch Lomond and the surrounding green countryside and rounded hills, and set a track for Stirling and Perthshire. Fifty-five minutes after leaving the Sheffield our wheels touched the runway at the Fleet Air Arm Base of Arbroath, where we stayed two days before flying to Twatt in the Orkneys. At Twatt we re-joined 700 Squadron, made up of crews of Walruses that were not at sea with their ships, and took part in anti-submarine patrols, communications flights & navigation exercises around Northern Scotland. We were still known as the "Sheffield Flight" throughout March and much of April though Z1761 had been withdrawn for an overhaul and we were using other aircraft. On 21st April Sub-Lieut. Stubbs was my observer in an anti-submarine patrol for the last time. Our flight was disbanded as our cruiser was undergoing an extensive refit and would not be putting to sea until mid-year, and then most of the ship's company would be different. At the end of April, I reported to 751 Squadron, R.N.A.S. Dundee, at Broughty Ferry to train observers whilst awaiting a further posting. Christopher was sent to the East Coast of America to join a squadron training on U.S. "Avenger" aircraft, & that squadron later embarked on an aircraft-carrier.

Tony's additional notes of interest pertaining to this account:

i) Many years later I read that the cyclone we had experienced had been recorded in the Admiralty as the fiercest in which a ship of the Royal Navy had been involved.

ii) After one or two letters in each direction, there was no news of Christopher during the war. Not for 38 years did we hear of each other. In 1981 my wife Phyllis and I were about to start a holiday in New Zealand (from N.S.W.) and it occurred to me that if Christopher had survived the war and fulfilled his ambition of becoming a doctor, his whereabouts should be known by the N.Z. Medical Association. It was, and since then we have revisited each other with our wives on several occasions.

iii) H.M.S. Sheffield was known as 'the Shiny Sheff' due to the unique strip of stainless steel around the edge of the deck, the gift of the steel city of Sheffield. The Master Cutlers of Sheffield also presented the wardroom with a stainless-steel table service.

iv) H.M.S. Sheffield was involved in all the important naval actions of the European zone during W.W.II; she had been part of the covering force for the Fleet Air Arm attack on the Italian Fleet in Taranto Harbour, had been with the ships searching for the "Bismark", and had taken a leading role in the Battle of the Barents Sea two months before we joined her—protecting Convoy JW 51B from the "Admiral Hipper" and the "Lutzow". On the 26th December, after our voyage in her, she was again in action in the Berents Sea, in the 'Battle of North Cape' in which H.M.S. Sheffield, two other medium cruisers and four destroyers attacked the battle-cruiser "Scharnhorst" of 32,000 tons (nine 11" guns) and caused her to run into the trap set by H.M.S. "Duke of York" (battleship) which sank the "Scharnhorst".

v) The catapult, across the deck between the funnels, needed the last few feet for deceleration, and so the aircraft accelerated from 0 to over 60 mph in about 65 feet.

Note: ALL THE PHOTOS of the seas were taken AFTER the cyclone, as the mist and sky were clearing a day or so later; it was impossible for the ship's photographer to take pictures during the storm itself—too dangerous as the spray and mist flying above the water prevented anything being seen.

(See images in Memorabilia Gallery in last chapter)

ROMANTIC SCOTLAND
(Anthea)

In England, on January 12th, 1921, my father was born to an unwed mother, who chose to place him for adoption when he was just a few days old. A loving English couple adopted him, and he was raised and educated in the city of Oxford, until he enlisted in the Royal Navy to serve his country during WWII.

As far as I know Dad had not left England prior to military service, although as a teenager and young man, he had often travelled within England, both on cycling trips and by train. After joining the Fleet Air Arm division of the Royal Navy, he was stationed at various bases in Great Britain, but also travelled to many places abroad. It seems that much of his service was at various bases in Scotland, where he also met my mother, who was serving in the Women's Royal Naval Service (WRNS: popularly and officially known as the Wrens).

Those who knew Dad well, would be quick to admit that in addition to all his other attributes, and his serious— at times almost melancholy demeanour—he enjoyed a good laugh, and could be quite light-hearted and humorous on occasion. He also possessed a romantic quality, a deep love for melodious music, and a passion to express his sensitive and romantic side through artwork and writing.

My father met and fell in love with my mother, Phyllis, while they were both stationed near Arbroath. After his various assignments upon his return, he would visit my mother and walk past the room where she worked, while whistling a "secret" tune, signalling to her that he was back from his mission. He would present her with beautiful drawings and loving sentiments on hand-made cards, some of which I have— and which I cherish. Tony and Phyllis were married in Glasgow and remained devoted to each other for the 71 years they were together. Here's a page

42

from one of the many beautiful letters Dad wrote to my mother. This one was written one month into their marriage.

I must share the following endearing story because it reveals a little-known fact—something very unusual. In wartime Britain, many commodities were scarce, or non-existent. One such item was wedding attire. Of course, the service men often wore their formal dress uniform, but bridal gowns for women were virtually unobtainable.

However, my mother was fortunate enough to wear a beautiful gown on her wedding day, thanks to First Lady Eleanor Roosevelt, who generously shipped a few gorgeous wedding dresses to Britain for the Wrens to wear on their special day. The gowns were passed around among brides serving in the Royal Navy. What a beautiful act of kindness on the First Lady's part.

Dad also fell in love with the rugged beauty of Scotland, particularly the Scottish Highlands. Long after wartime, my parents would vacation there and visit familiar places from the "old days", but they also travelled extensively to new sites, the Scottish Isles, visiting castles and lochs. Dad would photograph beautiful scenes, sketch the subject matter with notes on colours and details, then he would paint magnificent watercolour and oil paintings when they returned home.

The next story relates to a wartime event that ended well but certainly could have led to serious consequences. Although the account alludes to the potential for disaster, I feel my dad understated the severity of the actual situation, probably due to the safe ending. As you read the story, I think you may discern the gratitude felt by my father towards the R.A.F. personnel at

Tobermory Bay, Isle of Mull, who provided aid when it was greatly needed. A true port in the storm.

Clearly, Dad's memory of the assistance continued for many years, and each time he would hear Bing Crosby's 1954 song *Tobermory Bay*, the memory of that event would have rekindled his deep gratitude.

TOBERMORY BAY
(Tony)

On 19th October 1943 while stationed at Machrihanish in Kintyre, my duty was to fly Sub-Lt. Rolton (observer) and an air-gunner/telegraphist whose name is not recorded, on training exercises between Northern Ireland and the Inner Hebrides. We flew from Machrihanish in Walrus L2251 and alighted in Larne Harbour 45 minutes later. Then on northwards to Canna, Rhum and Skye being as far as our aircraft's range would allow. As we carried out navigational and other exercises the weather turned unpleasant—thick cloud and showers were accompanied by strong wind. When we turned south this wind was against us and reduced our effective speed across the water. Visibility continued to deteriorate for the low cloud descended almost to the water in places, and 100 ft. or so in others. When we could intermittently distinguish the rocky, irregular coast near the Sound of Arisaig it became necessary to fly low, 50 to 60 feet above the sea, to keep the shore in sight and check our position, when possible, under the sweeping expanses of mist and cloud.

After a period, not long in reality but seeming ages in those conditions, it became obvious that progress southward was being drastically slowed by the fierce headwind and the need to weave close to the coast while it could be seen. Thus, the question of fuel sufficiency arose. The distance to Machrihanish would have been within range of the aircraft on a calm day but the present circumstances of facing the wild wind and extremely poor visibility caused doubts to arise. We had been airborne a further 1 hour and 10 minutes from Larne so were nearly half-way through the fuel supply. Normally, the remaining half would have easily taken the plane to base—but this day, it would be touch and go. There was some reassurance in knowing that the Walrus was an amphibian floatplane which I was experienced in landing on the sea. However, if exhaustion of fuel brought that about, we would probably suffer a buffeting and hazardous spell in the stormy conditions at the mercy of tide and wind close to the craggy coast.

Losing sight of cliffs on our left we soon spotted land to our right, to the southwest, and immediately a small harbour appeared with a few little boats. A modest number of dwellings nestled around the northwest curve of the water. I thought perhaps we should take refuge there for the duration of the wild weather which could easily last two or more days. As we

45

circled around the harbour, we felt hopeful that our navigation and other clues had identified it correctly as Tobermory, Island of Mull. Two or three grey motorboats were moored near a jetty and a hut bearing a Royal Air Force (R.A.F.) flag, and some motor torpedo boats used for various purposes, including air-sea-rescue and reconnaissance. I landed the Walrus in the bay, and we moored near the M.T.B.'s (Motor Torpedo Boats).

R.A.F. personnel confirmed that this was Tobermory Bay. We explained our situation and were pleased to hear that the R.A.F. used similar octane petrol to ours, for the M.T.B.'s were powered by aircraft engines (Rolls Royce 'Merlins' I believe). A few 5-gallon drums of fuel were offered to us, and we struggled with these one at a time onto the upper wing of the plane. Unfortunately, there was no available method of transferring the petrol into the tanks other than by tilting the drums over the neck of the wing-tank, so that the spirit was exposed to the wind and vaporized in large measure, about 40 or 50 per cent being swept away in the blast. My companions and I improved our technique after the first drum, putting ourselves on the wind side of the process, using clothing to further shield the fuel and pouring as fast as possible. In due course we had managed to add 8-10 gallons to the tanks, certainly not a large amount but a precious addition when the fuel ratio to distance remaining would be critical, and we could not expect the R.A.F. people to forego any more of their limited supply.

We decided to take off and assess the prospect after flying 15 minutes, when it should not be difficult to return to Tobermory if things became threatening. Keeping at an extremely low altitude, it was possible to fly down the Sound of Mull and across the 4 or 5 miles of the Firth of Lorn to locate the islands and the jagged, irregular coastline of the mainland, and navigate a track into the Sound of Jura. There were several nasty moments when the cloud and rain obscured the view by descending below our own level or the indented shores fell away into the spray and mist. Negotiating the islands around Luing and Scarba took caution and a mixture of air navigation and map reading when any landmark became visible. Once above the Sound of Jura we were free of major obstructions and could proceed almost due south aiming for the Kintyre peninsular. By now there was a slight improvement in visibility and the outline of Kintyre was more even than the ragged areas northward, so once the peninsular was picked up we could keep relatively close to the shore and watch for familiar signs of the airbase at Machrihanish.

For much of this return journey there had been the alternative of flying high above the islands and hills and by navigating alone calculating when to descend over the water not far from base, but there was the problem of the fierce wind which was hard to estimate accurately for navigational purposes due to its varying direction and speed resulting from the very changeable nature of the land and sea areas. We could easily have been blown a few miles off track in such conditions, and if fuel ran out prior to reaching base this could happen over land, which would not be seen until our plane descended below the cloud. Trying to force-land a hull on rocky ground would be a hazardous procedure at the best of times. These were two of my reasons for deciding upon the alternative of keeping the surface of the sea and the shore in sight as much as possible. One hour and fifteen minutes after leaving Tobermory we landed on the runway at Machrihanish.

Whenever I hear the romantic song 'Tobermory Bay' (usually sung by Bing Crosby) I recall that small harbour and the R.A.F. base for motor torpedo boats in 1943.

ALL ABOARD!
(Anthea)

As I mentioned in an earlier chapter, my father was an ardent trainspotter from the time he was a young lad. He spent many hours at train stations studying steam engines as they pulled in and out of their platforms. Sometimes, he chose to lean over a railway bridge noting the train's characteristics as it clickety-clacked on the tracks below. As he ran hither and thither observing them and collecting pertinent information, he would record their engine numbers, and he knew the names of each locomotive. He could identify the different railway lines, and to which area of the country they travelled.

So knowledgeable was Dad regarding train routes in that era, he certainly would have known which stations one needed to embark or disembark for *any* destination in Southern England and beyond. While visiting train stations he would have had many encounters with those who worked for the railways such as station masters, platform guards, and signalmen, so he was well-acquainted with the routine workings of train systems. Indeed, this knowledge would have come in handy for him during this next escapade involving a passenger train.

I will confirm that Tony Shipperlee was a man of conviction and determination, and he always strived for perfection in anything and everything he tackled. Any task was performed in a superlative manner, with forethought, precision, and attention to detail. This due diligence prevailed throughout his life and was woven into the fabric of his very being. It is who he was. Never a stone left unturned. Never an "i" left undotted or a "t" uncrossed. Dad's work ethic and desire for perfection permeated all areas of his life, whether he was completing a mundane chore, finishing an oil painting, teaching his students, or executing a wartime duty.

I could communicate so many instances and examples to illustrate the kind of man my dad was, his determination, his perseverance and more, but I can exemplify the consistency of his temperament and character in the two examples shared below. Both accounts a) and b) occurred many years after the war but you will discover, as you read Tony's next two chapters involving incidents with WWII train travel, that whether it was in wartime, or at any time throughout his life, his actions and reactions remained consistent with his nature. Dad was predictably constant.

a) The first account takes us to Sydney, Australia during the mid-1960's. My parents had moved there for a 2-year tour when Dad left his position as Headmaster of Bicester Primary School in Oxfordshire after accepting a job as an elementary schoolteacher, in a suburb of Sydney. The position was a step down in seniority from being a headmaster, but Dad loved to travel, and Australia offered a warmer, sunnier climate. As I was married and living in California, there was nothing to deter them from the move. Funnily enough, although the contract was for only 2 years, they lived in Australia for 32 years, before returning to the UK to settle in Dorset.

To Tony's dismay, soon after arriving he discovered that to promote to a position in higher education, the Australian system would not accept his British qualifications, and required a degree from a University in Australia. This was indeed a low blow, but not a man to be thwarted, my father set a lofty goal—he would commit to a 4-year art course at Sydney University. That meant attending night courses after teaching in the classroom all day. Most weekends were consumed with painting subject matter and completing other required studies. From the first day of the course, my father adopted an attitude of *"I will show the blighters!"* He determined to finish top of his class—and yes, he did in fact graduate #1 that year. Later, his degree enabled him to enter the higher education system to teach art and craft as a college lecturer in Wollongong.

b) The second example happened on December 17th, 2017, only one month before he died. He had accepted an invitation to present his WWII flying experiences to The Wessex Strut Flying Club. After my mother died in July 2015, Dad and I would talk across the Atlantic by phone every day at approximately 8:30 am Texas time, so I was privy to his preparations for this talk. I marveled at the amount of time and effort he invested into his presentation—such attention to detail and just the right number of humorous moments inserted here and there. I felt it was a lot to take on for a man of 96 years, but in true form, he insisted on keeping his word and delivering the lecture. I later discovered that he stood for 90 minutes—refusing offers to sit down—as he addressed the audience and showed visuals to illustrate his points.

The talk was well received! How do I know? Well firstly because I know my dad well—as an accomplished storyteller and experienced lecturer who strove for excellence, he would have delivered an interesting presentation. Secondly, several people who had attended his December talk, took me aside at his funeral in late January 2018 and confirmed they had enjoyed his presentation. One of the gentlemen surprised me with a gift I will always treasure—a video recording of the entire presentation. What a meaningful gift—one that I cherish.

Here's the bottom-line regarding Dad. Whether an undertaking originated from his motivation, or under direction of a superior, whether the task was small, insignificant, or of great consequence, Tony Shipperlee utilized all his talents, determination, skill, and resourcefulness to complete the task at hand to the best of his ability. In other words, he gave his all.

In *Snap Decisions at Fareham,* my father's assignment came as a direct order from the Navy, a command that Dad took very seriously, as you will discover. As a side note, he admitted on a few occasions as he recounted the story, that his absolute resolve to fulfil the duty entrusted to him, emboldened his will, and prompted him to act as he did to bring the situation to a safe and satisfactory conclusion. At least once, as he laughed heartily in recollection of the incident, he declared that his snap decisions and the ensuing actions even surprised him!

In *Chance Circumstances,* Dad offers a glimpse into the range of emotions he felt as he encountered the nonsensical decisions of a railway official and the frustrations of wartime train travel on a snowy, wintry night. It is interesting how the weather inadvertently worked in Dad's favour. In a letter he wrote to me with the two train stories enclosed, he expressed the following .....

"The stories show how miraculous and unforeseen coincidences, or mistakes by humans or nature, can make a difference."

How very true.

TRAIN STORIES - SNAP DECISIONS AT FAREHAM
(Tony)

While serving at Ayr in a small two-pilot communications unit attached to the Admiral's Staff at Largs, our variety of land and amphibious planes received the addition of a twin-engined Airspeed Oxford. This necessitated Lieutenant Gareth Windsor or myself attending an 8-day course on multi-engined aircraft—and I was given this opportunity.

Thus, late in March 1944 I travelled to Lee-on-Solent and reported to Lieutenant Commander Hawley, commanding 762 Squadron, the Fleet Air Arm multi-engine unit. He greeted me enthusiastically, not because he was looking for someone to teach at that moment, but due to the shortage of staff to carry out a wholesale move of the squadron to Dale in South Wales.

"Ah!" he said, "We're having to transfer urgently to Pembrokeshire, and I only have one pilot for each plane to be flown there, with no officer left to take the maintenance and administrative personnel by rail, so you have solved my problem!"

The rail trip would be an all-day cross-country journey stopping at numerous large and small stations along the often picturesque, but tedious route, via Salisbury, Bristol area, the Severn Tunnel, Cardiff and across South Wales to the Haverfordwest-Milford Haven lines in far off Pembrokeshire. There we would be picked up by the squadron's road transport, already arrived with much of the stores and equipment, and taken the final 12 miles or more to Dale.

The following day or two were spent in continuing preparations for the move, while I enjoyed a few periods of leisure and wondered at the situation that entangled me. Much later it became apparent that the likely cause of this outfit's transfer was the build-up on the South Coast of fighter squadrons in readiness for the D-Day landing about 10 weeks later.

Early on the morning of departure I was given a railway warrant for the journey of the Squadron personnel, comprising a Chief Petty Officer, several Petty Officers and Leading Hands, maintenance crews and a few Wrens. The airplanes had already been loaded with some essential equipment and stores and were ready for flying.

It had been arranged by some higher Naval authority that a special carriage should be attached to the rear of a regular scheduled train leaving Portsmouth for South Wales, and that our party should board this reserved coach at Fareham, 5 miles from Lee-on-Solent. On alighting from the road vehicles, the personnel were checked and assembled near that end of the platform where the appropriate coach was to stop.

A short while later the train drew into Fareham Station. However, no notices could be seen on the rear carriage and, like the others, showed members of the public spread throughout the compartments.

This required my immediate investigation, as the train was scheduled for only a short stop. To my alarm, neither the train guard nor the platform porter, had any knowledge of the reserved coach. Fifty yards or so beyond the locomotive was the signal box, and the exit signal went down indicating permission for the driver to move off whenever the guard waved his green flag—and *this* guard was impatient to do so. Obviously, I could not delay some effective action, or departing carriages would leave the naval contingent behind, requiring some embarrassing explanation to my superiors later. Either that or the personnel would have to scramble aboard hastily, ending in ones and twos scattered along the length of the train.

Both unthinkable situations demanded to be avoided by a third alternative thought up swiftly on the spot. Therefore, I sent a Petty Officer across to the Stationmaster's office on the far platform, informing him of the nonappearance of the expected coach and requesting his presence on this platform to solve the problem. Simultaneously, I dispatched a Petty Officer to the footplate to politely explain the position to the driver, and another to the signalman in the box. The nearby guard was informed that we would cause only the minimum of hold up necessary.

Within moments there appeared a stocky middle-aged man wearing the uniform topcoat and cap of the Stationmaster. Unfortunately, instead of the pleasant co-operation hoped for, it was clear immediately this railway official was taking an indignant and aggressive posture. He pitched straight in with a demand to know why the train was not already out of the station and why we had any right to delay it.

I tried explaining that the naval group were supposed to be provided with a separate carriage, to remain as a unit, and the best thing would be for us all to solve the problem amiably. For instance, we could wait while a spare coach from one of those in his siding was connected. This response drew an ill-humoured response to the effect that none of those coaches was spare, it being Portsmouth's job to provide one and since this had not been forthcoming, we would have to find places among the passengers wherever we could. Such an idea was unsuitable, for as I explained to the Stationmaster, on the long trip to Pembrokeshire there would be repeated temptations at the many stops for one or more of the personnel to alight from the train and perhaps end up missing, and we could not risk that.

This drew only another unhelpful remark from this officious person, who was obviously not used to tolerating suggestions from his staff and treated them in a domineering fashion. A last attempt was made to persuade him to solve the difficulty by asking passengers in the rear coach to move to vacant seats further forward. At this he flared into a temper shouting that this would take too much time and the train was already late, so we must put up with whatever seating we could find and be quick about it or he would order the railway staff to move the train on its way. I remember his last explanation well and, for me, it was the last straw as he blurted out,

"You people must put up with the inconvenience like everyone else—don't you know there's a war on?"

I responded, "Indeed, we do more than many people like yourself, but right now you are about to discover that war has reached this station!"

"Chief!" I said, turning to the petty Officer, "take a Leading Wren and together work your way along the rear carriage politely asking all the passengers to relocate in empty seats further forward. Explain we regret the necessity, but we have no alternative since the railway has not provided the coach arranged by the navy. Assure them that a sailor will help anyone with a heavy case."

54

Two men with rifles were sent to join the Petty Officer at the locomotive with orders not to allow it to commence motion, in case the Stationmaster had ideas of ranting at the crew.

By now the remaining Navy men and women still in lines were thoroughly enjoying the altercation which was providing momentary entertainment in an otherwise tiring day for them.

I had not been expecting a problem such as the one that had arisen but felt obliged to solve it quickly and decisively. Having realized that we meant business, the Stationmaster lapsed into threats such as:

"I'll report this to railway authorities."

I tried to reply calmly, "I hope you do, then they can explain to the Admiralty why the carriage was not supplied, and the local Stationmaster was obstructive and abusive to Naval personnel trying to carry out wartime duties!"

No unpleasantness would have arisen if we had had a more congenial approach from the station bully.

Within minutes the carriage was empty, and it was pleasing to hear that the passengers involved had been understanding and helpful. The Wrens were sent together to one compartment and the men seated in suitable groups under the care of Petty Officers or Leading Hands. I walked to the driver and expressed regrets at the hold up. He and his fireman were enjoying a leisurely smoke and mildly amused by the events.

We puffed away from the platform. At length, late in the day, we reached our destination in the far west of Wales, after hours of big town stops, small country halts and much attractive scenery, with all the company present and everything in order.

No further word was ever heard of this incident.

In this note, handwritten at the end of his typed story, Dad expresses some thoughts:

Just the anecdote about the train affair in March, 1944.
Not a great war-winning event, but a rather unusual
experience, & reflection of what one of your children's
ancestors used to be like, since they still seem
interested in these things.   The one thing that
appears different to me on reading it myself (from
the days in 1944) is that then I felt very "adult," confident,
experienced & mature, but now I realise that I
was only 23 & 2 months — surprise to me at this
ripe old age.   Love, Dad

TRAIN STORIES- CHANCE CIRCUMSTANCES
(Tony)

Between early 1942 and early 1946 I made numerous rail journeys from southern England to Scotland or the reverse. Once from the west coast of Scotland to Oxford, the overnight express from Glasglow to London was due to stop only at Lancaster and Crewe. At London it was then necessary to cross via the underground tube system to Paddington to catch another train to Oxford, adding around two hours to the time of arrival in London, as well as humping cases up and down escalators and along tunnels. About forty minutes before London was a junction at Bletchley where every ninety minutes or so a stopping train ran across country direct to Oxford. When trains stopped at Bletchley, therefore, the total time saved was anything from one to two hours and the last part of the trip was much more convenient. This express was not scheduled to stop anywhere after Crewe.

It was a winter's night, cold and dark, and the wartime blackout meant keeping the blinds down. At about midnight the other two people in my compartment of six seats settled down to sleep, the lights being dim or off. Soon afterwards I dozed off, waking when the train halted at Crewe and sampling a cup of wartime railway tea. The tea, at major junctions like Crewe and York, was constantly in demand as trains full of servicemen and women were arriving and departing frequently, twenty-four hours per day. This tea was dark brown, thick, and stale, tasting as though brewed from old rotting socks, and usually devoid of enough milk to moderate its strength. Although gulped down by mouths suffering from the effects of stuffy, overcrowded, blacked-out carriages, the tea was nevertheless a subject of scorn and comment. It was widely believed that the brew did not result so much from need to economize in tea leaves as from the continuous surge of people against the counter not allowing the attendants time to empty, clean and refill the large urn, or completely replace it by another—for more tea was added to an existing half-full container and topped up with boiling water, the process being repeated ad infinitum.

After Crewe I fell asleep again. On rousing soon after 5 a.m. I lifted a corner of the blind and peered into the gloom. It was still dark, but snow had fallen and this white covering lying everywhere made it possible to just distinguish dimly silhouetted shapes—shapes that indicated an industrial area and railway centre. I felt some appeared slightly familiar. No, it was not yet London outskirts. *Could it be Bletchley?* It did not look like it. I stared at other faint masses as the train slowed—it must be one of the larger rail centres north of Bletchley, such as Stafford or Rugby. I was sure I had seen these shapes previously. As the train continued slowing, it was possible to distinguish the end of a platform, so I hastily lifted down my case and hurried along the corridor to the door in case an opportunity came to exit at a convenient station. There was just sufficient light from the dimmed lamps under the roof to make out the name—Rugby! Excellent, the train was coming to a standstill.

Not waiting to ponder the reason for this unscheduled stop, I opened the door and lifted my baggage onto the platform. As I did so, a station official was hurrying towards a coach further along the train and calling to someone also climbing from a door,

"This is not a scheduled stop! Passengers cannot get off here."

I thought the passenger was wearing an army officer's uniform. He began speaking to the railwayman who became argumentative and aggressive. So, I hastened thirty or forty feet to a dark doorway of an office and did my best to lurk in the shadows with my luggage out of sight, hoping that the locomotive would hurry up and steam away. It did, and to my amazement the army man was climbing aboard and went off with it. The station official was turning round, and from his slightly bent stance and general posture, I could sense his lingering feeling of uncertainty as to whether the soldier had been tempted to resist his authority—and then the railwayman's growing mixture of relief and satisfaction resulting from his successful persuasion. He shuffled towards the buildings and stiffened up as though reacting to the realization that he had maintained his authority.

"What a piece of stupidity." I thought. "What difference could it make to the official or the railway if a couple of passengers were fortunate enough to be able to leave the train at a more convenient place than London, from where some would then have to travel part of the way back."

I wondered if the army chap had really wanted to depart or if he was just stretching his legs or making an inquiry. From the discussion and the attitude of the official I concluded he must have wanted to get off.

I vowed that under no threats would that station fellow pressure me into boarding a train that did not suit my plans, especially as the one from

Scotland had now steamed well clear of the station. I squeezed further into the shadows as the official entered an adjoining office. After a few moments I moved in the opposite direction and saw dim lights through windows—a canteen, with a woman attending to the tea urn and a glass case of sandwiches and buns. Caution indicated that I must not draw attention to my presence yet. Ah, another entrance, the men's toilets. I moved inside and made myself scarce for several minutes. It sounded as though another train stopped but I couldn't be sure. I hoped so, because then perhaps it would be assumed I had come from that one. Perhaps it would look like I'd entered from the street, but I did not know where that entrance was or if it was guarded by a ticket office. Venturing into the lighted area I entered the canteen as naturally as I could.

"Are you serving?" I enquired. It was around six a.m.

"Just opened, Ducks. What do you want?" the jolly server asked.

I thought I had better have a bun and one of the abominable cups of tea. It wasn't too bad and obviously was the first brew of the day. While I sat at a table the same railway official entered. There didn't seem to be other passengers around, so probably no train had stopped a few minutes before, or perhaps it had been a goods train. The railwayman nodded to me. How could he have missed seeing me get off the Scottish express? He must have been too intent on turning back the other fellow. Anyway, he made no sign of recognition. I now felt safe enough to ask if a train stopping at Bletchley were due soon.

"The one after next," he informed me.

My curiosity caused me to ask if the long train, leaving as I reached the station about fifteen minutes earlier, had been going to stop at Bletchley. The official was eager to impart the news that it certainly was not and should not have stopped at Rugby and no one had been permitted to disembark. I mentally thanked the army man for holding the station official's attention so well.

"Why did the train stop?" I risked.

"Because the signal failed to operate. Overnight snow had lodged in the mechanism and a frozen lump had stopped the arm moving which covered the green light and left the red showing. When the train was forced to halt a signalman climbed the framework and hacked away the snow, so that the arm could indicate 'Go'."

What a series of chance circumstances, I pondered—just happening in this station and not somewhere along the many miles of open country, and my waking at the right moment. And knowing the rail system well enough to anticipate a connection to Bletchley and thence direct to Oxford.

JUSTICE AND FAIR PLAY
(Anthea)

I thought it appropriate to entitle this book *Planes, Trains and War Games* because a few of Dad's wartime escapades might seem mischievous or a bit on the carefree side. Considering the seriousness of WWII, in no way do I wish to misconstrue the horrors of war or give any illusion that I (or my dad) might associate such hostilities with any sort of frivolous game. Nonetheless, I find it enlightening that, despite the obvious devastation, suffering, and carnage that accompany a world at war, the *Greatest Generation* was, in large part, comprised of young, enthusiastic, young men and women who seemingly attempted to live life passionately, making the best of those frightening and uncertain times.

They served their country, risked their lives to win the war, fought valiantly for freedom, and as battles raged on, circumstances undeniably instilled them with an urgency to live life in the finest way possible—while they still had the chance. Life is not guaranteed at any time, but during war, the odds of dying young increase dramatically. One can understand that priorities would naturally realign as the uncertainty of one day to the next became painfully evident. I imagine they lived and loved, they fought fiercely, and they played hard whenever circumstances permitted. They mourned for their dead comrades and the state of the world, they viewed their commitments seriously but they also enjoyed an off-duty party, and a fun prank with friends now and then. Britain and the allies *had* to win, and everyone involved had a part to play.

In Great Britain, millions of posters with three different slogans were printed by the government, calling for persistence in the face of challenge. *Your Courage, Your Cheerfulness, Your Resolution; Will Bring Us Victory.* Another read, *Freedom is in Peril; Defend it with all Your Might.* The population was urged to *Keep Calm and Carry On!* I'm told that most of the posters were never placed but remained hidden away until they were discovered in 1940.

The last of the slogans seems very relevant. As my father describes, the British kept calm and carried on with courage and dignity, and they embraced any sense of intermittent normalcy, even though nothing about life was normal during WWII. Life as they knew it had changed forever. But their values prevailed, and perhaps those attributes might even have strengthened due to hardships they faced. I refer to specific characteristics attributed to people who were born in 1901-1927, the *Greatest Generation*—an age bracket who upheld the standards of integrity, humility, work ethic, service, loyalty, fair play, justice, personal responsibility, and commitment.

At the beginning of the book, written in *Boys Will Be Boys* as background to Dad's choirboy story, you will recall that I highlighted a few of the boys' characteristics that would prove helpful to them later in life. I spoke of mischievous and bold behaviour, but I also emphasized they were strong defenders of such values as fair play, integrity, and justice. My father was the ultimate crusader for fair play and justice.

Just as the beliefs of the young choirboys prompted bold actions to set right an injustice, so you will also discover the very same beliefs were instrumental in escalating this next incident. Indignation at unfair treatment can precipitate bold attempts to correct perceived injustices. Please note also the prevalence of mischievous behaviour!

SAILS, SADDLES AND CHAINS
(Tony)

While the small aircraft-carrier H.M.S. Emperor was anchored in the Alexandria Harbour, Egypt, for occasional periods in October 1944, the usual practice of using "liberty boats" was followed. Groups of off-duty crewmen could board a small launch and be taken to a jetty for a period ashore. The ship anchored well out in the large harbour, and it would take the liberty boat several minutes to reach land. It would then take on any crew who were waiting to return to the ship. Sometimes it would depart at half-hour intervals, or at times, more often. Although an hourly schedule could exist, leaving at specific times, arrangements depended on circumstances and the time of day.

By that stage of the war, bananas were almost unobtainable in Britain, and it was therefore a novelty to munch two or three in Alexandria. Another treat was visiting one of the excellent French restaurants to indulge in the special pastries produced in these patisseries, then walk along the main road overlooking the harbour, in the warm Mediterranean sunshine.

In company with another pilot, I joined a liberty boat late one afternoon and enjoyed a couple of hours of luxury difficult to obtain in the late autumn of wartime England. When we returned to the jetty, we saw the liberty boat well out on its way to the ship. Two marines told us that it would be quite some while (about 45 minutes I think) before another launch would arrive at the pick-up point, and they had decided to hire a felucca—a small sailing vessel of the Mediterranean or large rowboat. This was easy as there were always plenty available, with their owners waiting to take liberty men back to the ships and collect payment.

The four of us decided to share a boat, so we approached the group of Egyptians squatting about thirty yards away on the stone apron overlooking the boats in the inner harbour. One of the men indicated that he owned a particular boat, a little larger than many, and pointing to it, held out his hand for payment from each of us. The money having passed to him, he remained on the ground, announcing in a type of broken-English, with words missing from phrases, that he would *need more people to pay for the boat,* but he was able to assure us by his gestures, facial expressions, and skeleton sentences, that he would not keep us more than a few minutes. This was believable as a trickle of men wound its way fairly frequently to the jetty to return to ships. We sat in the boat and waited. After about ten minutes two sailors joined us. We all waited about three more minutes, then decided to inform the Egyptian that he now had enough passengers to cast off. Two went with this information but he was greedy for more shillings or piastres and intimated his intention to wait for more sailors. He felt in control since he had already collected the fares.

Within two more minutes, as there was no one in sight who looked a bit like a prospective passenger, we six agreed that we had waited long enough, too long in fact, and this unscrupulous individual should be jolted into action in some way and given a fright. We planned to achieve this by commencing to paddle and row the vessel away from the jetty. If the greedy owner hurried to the small pier and showed panic and willingness to take the boat to the ship, we would move in shore and pick him up, but circumstances would have to influence our response, as threats would probably persuade us to make our own way to the "Emperor" and let him rescue his vessel by going out in one of his companions' boats. It took perhaps a minute to finalize details of the getaway. At a given signal, one of us would untie a rope holding the craft to the jetty, another would cast off the painter looped over a post, and the others would pick up paddles and oars and energetically start moving the vessel. Perhaps it would be necessary for a few pushes on the bottom of the comparatively shallow water with one or more oars to get the boat underway.

Simultaneously we sprang to our positions and individual tasks, mine being to disengage one of the lines securing the craft. It was a heavier, more cumbersome felucca than any others, more like a large whaler, though I seem to visualize it being fatter in the bottom and squarer at the stern. It handled sluggishly but we nosed it out a few feet and all seemed to be proceeding as planned.

The Egyptian leaped to his feet and ran towards us, shouting and gesticulating, followed by half a dozen companions. As he reached the edge of the platform, he jumped into the water which was not too deep to stand on the bottom. Two or three others joined him, and half strode, half swam, towards the felucca. We believed we could thwart their attempts to reach us by paddling and rowing hard, putting an adequate distance between them and the boat, pushing off any who reached the gunwales. Once we were twenty yards or more from land, it would be unlikely the Egyptians, mostly fat and middle-aged, could catch the vessel, and the harbour water would soon be too deep and too choppy for easy swimming.

We appeared to be progressing nicely when our confidence was quickly replaced by alarm and dismay. We had crossed fifteen to eighteen feet of water when a chain rose to the surface, in a line from the stern to the jetty, then a second splashed into view. They had been lying on the bottom and attached below the water level. Now they were stretched along the surface taking the strain of the heavy boat's surge seaward and suddenly jolting it to a stop. There was no time to puzzle out the means of disconnecting them for a couple of the Egyptians were already pulling themselves up the landward gunwale and two others were reaching the stern. Pushing their shoulders failed to dislodge them and two or three were drawing ugly looking knives. I saw three of my companions striking the boarding locals with oars and paddles and realized this affair was becoming serious, threatening and potentially dangerous.

About sixty yards inshore a whistle blew, then two or three more sounded, as nine or ten figures in dilapidated uniforms came from a hut and began streaming towards the jetty, with half a dozen boatmen trailing behind. Shouting and waving excitedly, this motley group spread along the platform. By then, the first attacker managed to climb inboard and struggled with a sailor, while a marine was dealing more paddle blows upon a second assailant half across the gunwale. Shouts from the harbour police and commands from the one in charge influenced the felucca proprietors for they withdrew from the fight and climbed ashore. For the latter half of the two or three minutes of the conflict I had been desperately struggling with hands under water to free the chained boat, believing that if we could move further out, we would have the advantage. Unfortunately, the chains were fastened too securely in some obscure manner. I recall that they seemed to be permanently nailed to the vessel and joined about three feet out of reach with the ends from the seabed or jetty posts. Maybe the owner had experienced this trouble before. Most likely he made a habit of taking payment, then keeping passengers waiting for additional customers. Certainly, there was plenty of thieving in Egypt, and probably boats were liable to disappear.

With the vessel securely fixed at the 15 to 18 feet from the landing stage we had no avenue of escape. There was no hope of swimming half a mile or more to the aircraft carrier, and no small boat was close enough for us to transfer to another. The police and boatmen lined themselves along the landing area as the senior policeman argued with the owner of the felucca and shouted instructions all around. Then, as the boatmen quietened down momentarily, he spoke in passable English to us. I do not remember the detailed wording, but I know we did not agree to moving the boat landward until we were convinced that the police officer would be able to control the excitable and aggressive boatmen. Once we stepped on land, the senior policeman insisted that we went to his shed so that he could write particulars of the incident. He was in an officer's uniform, aged in his thirties and conscious of his superior standing among the other Egyptians. He clearly endeavoured to preserve his dignity and remain aloof from his countrymen and was keen to maintain respect from all there.

I remember a fairly heated argument ensuing at first, as the felucca owner insisted on punishment for the British Naval personnel and financial compensation for himself. The noisy discussion at one stage brought threats of retaliation from both sides. As the senior member of the British group, I found myself the spokesman, a role I probably was not reluctant to take, being at the age of twenty-three, a rather outspoken and energetic proponent of "justice and fair play." There was talk of holding us at the police post, whereupon I demanded a telephone line to the Royal Navy HQ on shore and put forward the notion of dire penalties for local officials preventing allied servicemen from joining their ship. I again stressed the fact that all six had paid the felucca man but had not yet received the service he had offered.

I detected in the officer of police some misgivings about pushing charges upon us yet concern not to lose face with his countrymen by appearing not to fully support their case. He was approaching the stage of being in a quandary. Somehow, and I cannot recall precise details now unfortunately, I was able to talk him into seeing our point of view and dampening down the demands of the boat owner and persuading him to inform his subordinates that he had no jurisdiction over British Naval personnel. After all, the violence had begun by the boat crews. By the time he hesitatingly gave orders that no one should detain us, and we walked back to the jetty, the next liberty boat could be seen approaching the wharf and several more sailors and marines gathered in readiness to board it. I believe we all discreetly mingled with them and were content to "call it a day." Two of our companions were nursing bumps and bruises but satisfied to muse on the antics of the boat proprietor and the surprises, and trouble, as well as the wetting he had received. An amusing, but serious lesson for another of his ilk was to follow within a few days.

Two or three days after the incident above, a small group of friends were with me on the walkway just below the flight deck, looking over the

66

rail towards Alexandria. We were relaxing and enjoying the wide harbour scene while awaiting the time to go below for the next meal. Several cargo vessels and warships were scattered in various directions, all at anchor. Triangular sails of a few small feluccas showed up against the grey-green sea. Spray and wake from two or three motorboats added splashes of white, while here and there other small craft provided further variety.

One small felucca, tacking to gain advantage from the modest breeze, was slowly nearing H.M.S. Emperor. Before long, two occupants could be distinguished. One was the Egyptian sailing the boat and the other was a naval officer. They gradually drew closer, and one friend recognized the passenger as "Max". Max was at times referred to as Mad Max and The Wild Irishman due to his frequently wild, adventurous ways, and because he was from the Emerald Isle. As a Southern Irishman whose county was neutral, Max need not have been in the war but had chosen to fight with the British. Although I did not know him well, I had talked with him on a few occasions, and he seemed a likeable fellow. I could see that underlying his rather relaxed manner in normal conversation there was a more energetic, impetuous temperament that might easily rise to the fore.

In the succeeding minutes while we idly gazed on the general view, the felucca sailed even closer. There was a gangway of steps on the outside of the ship and the normal procedure was for a boat to draw alongside the small platform at the bottom of this stairway. The felucca was quietly and smoothly being manoeuvred into position to reach the gangway, still about twenty feet away, when the occupants sprang to their feet, raising their voices. A noisy argument developed with the Egyptian brandishing a large, curved knife. Almost immediately, the two figures engaged in a violent tussle. When they parted, we could see that Max had the evil weapon and the felucca man was backing away. The Irishman made a move in his direction and the Egyptian turned and scampered towards the bow. Max pursued him and after a quick flight around the vessel the Egyptian jumped at the lower mast and scrambled up far enough to be out of the pursuer's reach unless he followed. Max did not follow but took the tiller and somehow managed to guide the boat close enough to the platform for someone on duty there to pull on the boathook or oar extended by Max and bring the felucca alongside. As Max climbed upwards, he threw the knife towards the boat, now drifting away. My recollection is that the weapon hit the sea and disappeared. We were treated to a spectacle of the Egyptian climbing down his own mast to regain control of the felucca, ejaculating shouts of abuse as he headed back towards the city.

Max informed us that the not unfamiliar event had occurred just before they reached the ship. The felucca owner demanded more money, or he would turn the small vessel around. Max had retorted in angry terms, so the boat owner had drawn his long-bladed knife. We had witnessed The Wild Irishman living up to his reputation.

MEMORIES OF MELOS
(Anthea)

My father did not talk about his wartime encounters much—at least not to me. I suspect that behind closed doors, he and my mother had conversations from time to time, perhaps remembering their shared experiences. Since they both were in branches of the Royal Navy, stationed in Scotland during their courtship, I know they enjoyed plenty of happy times together leading up to their wedding and early months of marriage, despite forced wartime separations and the accompanying worries.

It wasn't until years after the war that Dad started writing the stories shared in this book. One by one, he would mail these stories to me, having compiled them with frequent reference to his navy log books for accuracy of dates and events, and from notes and photographs he had kept in folders. His photographic memory would certainly have helped as well. The two stories that follow were the last of the WWII stories he wrote. They detail the facts, his thoughts, and observations surrounding the attack on Melos, in which he played a significant role.

I believe of all his wartime recollections, the attack on Melos impacted Dad the most. The memory of it quietly haunted him for years. The full consequences of bombardments directed against the enemy, based on his spotting and coordinates, resulted in massive explosions targeting the German garrison. Not knowing the casualty count and extent of lives impacted, particularly any civilian losses, certainly took its toll on him and, on the few occasions my father spoke of those events, he was highly emotional. In Part One of the Melos Attack, Dad briefly mentions his concerns for the number of lives lost. Thoughts of the attack deeply disturbed him—more than his account indicates. So much so, that sixty years later he took actions that brought forth what Dad considered was a happy conclusion to years of wondering, feelings of melancholy, and self-imposed guilt.

In October of 2004, my parents, who loved to travel, visited the Greek Island of Melos for a holiday, with more in mind than sunshine and beautiful scenery. My father wished to visit historic locations on the island where the Germans had been encamped, and where their guns were placed—the very ones that had fired at my father's Swordfish* as he and his observer flew reconnaissance maneuvers around Melos on 26th October 1944. He hoped to perhaps meet someone on Melos who might provide insight as to what had transpired on the ground because of the bombardment.

Thanks to my father's tenacity and his ability to start friendly conversations with complete strangers, his enquiries led to a complicated series of events that ended in his meeting individuals in Melos who were able to direct him to the wartime sites he sought to visit. In addition, he met a resident of Melos by the name of John Scarvelis. He and Dad became friends, and subsequently they corresponded for many years. My father writes the following in his notes,

"John stressed the importance of Melos to the Germans, as a base and port of call for supply ships taking equipment to Tobruk for the African Corps. He and others indicated that very few Germans were killed by the bombardment on October 26th and thought it very unlikely that any local residents were injured when the ammunition dump blew up because the German military installations were in isolated parts away from residents and guarded so that no locals would be allowed near."

This information would have alleviated my father's concerns about the numbers of casualties and provided him with welcome relief from years of wondering about the aftermath of the attack. The greatest discovery from his visit to Melos was learning that one of the German Officers stationed there in 1944 had grown fond of the island and later purchased a house there, where he returned for frequent holidays. This German officer was Snr. Lt. Horst Seegers, the Freya radar commander.

The story becomes even more interesting at this point. My father was able to establish telephone contact with Herr Seegers from information provided by individuals in Melos. While Dad never met Herr Seegers in person, they did converse several times by telephone, and they regularly corresponded by mail. They shared their wartime incidents and during the first phone call Dad asked,

"Do you remember when you were in Melos, you fired on a spotter aircraft? And the spotter aircraft got the guns of the ship

70

aimed on you?" Herr Seegers vaguely remembered. Dad continued, "Well, I was the pilot, and this is a friendly talk. It's 60 years later and I don't have any anger, I'm just curious to know a few things!" And so, they talked. He confirmed that two Germans had died in the attack that day, and no civilians.

The following year, my parents visited Crete and were able to meet one of Herr Seegers three daughters and family. They enjoyed their time together. A week after returning home from Crete, my father received a phone call from Mrs. Seegers, Horst's wife, who spoke very good English. Here is what she said,

"Tony, I must tell you this. My daughter phoned her father and said, '*Dad, I'm so glad you didn't shoot him down, as he's such a nice man!*'"

As I mentioned, Dad rarely spoke of this event but on the two occasions I heard him tell the story, emotions took over, and he choked back tears. I am so grateful that a happy conclusion brought my father a sense of peace and redemption.

*Note: The Fairey Swordfish was a frontline attack aircraft used by the Fleet Air Arm of the Royal Navy in WWII. This 1930's torpedo bomber biplane was slow and outdated. It was a dive-bomber, could perform night missions and, notably, it pioneered the use of Air to Surface Vessel (ASV) radar. It was nicknamed "Stringbag" in comparison to the string shopping bags commonly used by shoppers at the time—the nickname intended to be complimentary since the bag had the ability to carry an improbable combination of loads.

The following quote regarding the Swordfish aircraft is from The Aviation History Online Museum:

"Despite being antiquated, it sank more tonnage than any other Allied plane during the World War II and served from the beginning of the war until the end. Of its most famous missions, it played a role in the attack of the strategic Italian port of Taranto and it made a critical strike that led to the sinking of the most famous of all German battleships, the Bismarck."

THE ATTACK ON MELOS: PART ONE
(Tony)

A small naval force glided from Alexandria Harbour into the Mediterranean during the night of 24th October 1944 and sailed north-westward. The following day, near Crete, my warrant officer observer and I carried out a radio telegraphy test in Swordfish No.170, returning to the ship by means of a deck landing; five landings on the flight deck had been carried out for practice the previous day. As dawn broke on 26th October, the small group of vessels approached the Greek Island of Melos (sometimes spelled Milos); the group included the cruiser H.M.S. Aurora, about two destroyers, and our 'escort' carrier H.M.S. Emperor of 11,400 tons, built in Seattle-Tacoma and commissioned in August 1943. The 'Emperor' was one of an American series of such vessels converted during construction from merchant ship design to 'flat-top' with a hanger underneath to hold twenty to thirty aircraft with wings folded and taken below by means of a lift. The hull was of welded type, total length 494 feet, driven by a single propeller and capable of the modest speed of 18 knots.

Melos was roughly mid-way between Crete and the Greek mainland, 75 miles approximately from the nearest mainland spurs. News had reached British Headquarters in the Eastern Mediterranean that the commander of the German garrison occupying Melos had realized the war was lost for the Nazis and wanted to surrender. The information had come through Greek resistance patriots on the island.

The purpose of our expedition, known as Force B, was to steam close to the island showing warships and aircraft. By dropping thousands of leaflets from low-flying planes we would demonstrate the ability to attack the garrisons of 1200 soldiers. The leaflets, in German, stressed that other Nazi garrisons on the islands had already given up and that unnecessary conflict and casualties would be avoided if the Melos soldiers also laid down their arms. The war would then be over for them. The intelligence reports led to the belief that the leaflets and the sight of the warships and aircraft would convince any hesitant members of the garrison that prolonging war in that area was futile and would result in needless death. To take the soldiers into custody and round up any stragglers or dissidents, 600 commandos were aboard the ships, ready to storm ashore.

72

The leaflet-dropping planes were met with some resistance in the form of machine-gun fire and anti-aircraft shells. On one of the leaflet missions a Hellcat fighter-bomber from H.M.S. Emperor was hit and its pilot was forced to bale out. He settled in shallow water in an obscure bay and was quickly picked up by the carrier's Walrus amphibian aircraft piloted by Lieut. Issaverdens. "Izzy" was the only other seaplane pilot (besides me) in our expedition. The arrangement was that he, with observer, would crew the air-sea-rescue Walrus one day while I and my observer flew the Swordfish to spot for the cruiser's guns, and we would change aircraft on alternate days. As things worked out, Izzy did virtually no "spotting" and I was not called on for air-sea-rescue as the need did not arise on an appropriate date.

A short conference had been held aboard H.M.S. Aurora at which ships' captains and commanders of destroyers met the senior gunnery officers and 'spotter aircraft' crews and discussed procedures and detailed targets. We were issued with maps of Melos showing several targets labelled A, B, C, and so forth. The main ones were a garrison headquarters, a battery of coastal guns (about 5 in.) and a battery of 88mm. anti-aircraft guns. I was reassured to hear the "Aurora's" Captain tell us 'Spotter' personnel that as the cruiser would be firing over a range of hills most of the time at targets thus out of sight, it was essential that the aircraft spotting facility be preserved, so that if anti-aircraft fire endangered us, we should ask for salvos to be directed against the 88mm. battery.

My observer, a regular navy warrant officer, was 34 years of age. I was then 23 years old. He had the nickname of 'Drunkie'—for obvious reasons. We had been to Alexandria together several times enjoying French cakes and bananas which were almost unobtainable in wartime Britain, and Drunkie had indulged in adequate quantities of spirits. He explained that he was able to minimize his fears about forthcoming action by numbing his senses a little. He told me something of his background, including his occasional visits to his sister in St. Matthews district of Oxford, an area I knew from childhood, and would be teaching near there a few years later.

Since the response to the invitation to surrender was hostile, the decision was made to use the squadron of Hellcats to drop small bombs on the main targets and to position the ships for bombardment by "Aurora". I believe each Hellcat could take off with one 250-pound bomb underneath. Hellcats were American made single wing planes with a squat, almost barrel-like fuselage, due to the large round engine at the nose. A pilot was the only occupant. Our British Walrus was a comparatively small cabin-hull amphibian. With wheels retracted under the lower wing it could land on and take off from water. With wheels down it could land on decks & runways, so was very versatile, especially as it was also fitted with stubs for being catapulted off warships equipped with the appropriate mechanism. Its normal crew was three—pilot, observer, and radio-air gunner. As the Walrus was being reserved for air-sea-rescue, a Swordfish biplane was aboard for spotting purposes. This plane could carry a torpedo as Swordfish had done at Taranto early in the naval war with Italy when a daring night raid had immobilized important units of the Italian fleet. A crew was usual—in our case two were adequate for observing the fall of shot and reporting to the gunnery officer of the ship involved.

When H.M.S. Aurora was positioned to begin firing at the enemy headquarters, we flew off the "Emperor" in Swordfish 170. For some reason that is hard to explain I had chalked a large '13' on the side of the fuselage, maybe from some feeling of bravado or to convince Drunkie or myself when we returned safely that any superstition was unfounded. Whatever had prompted the chalked number, it brought surprised looks from maintenance and deck crews. Perhaps half an hour elapsed before we had surveyed the territory from 7000 feet, checked the communications equipment with the cruiser and were informed that a single smoke-bomb was to be fired to test the range. It would be a six-inch shell as the main armament of the "Aurora" was six 6-inch guns mounted in three twin-turrets. The ship had been armed also with eight 4-inch dual-purpose guns. It displaced 5,270 tons, was 480 feet long & 51 ft. in the beam and had been built at Portsmouth Dockyard in 1936. A few months before the Melos episode it had been engaged in extensive bombardment of the Normandy coastal emplacements prior to the 'D-Day' landings. The gunnery officer had told me that the rifling of the barrels was worn which might result in less accuracy than he would like.

My companion had already pulled out his flask of brandy, adding to the liquid he had consumed before being airborne. Soon after the cruiser began ranging single shots to find its first target several grey and black puffs, like miniature clouds, appeared in front of us, hovering briefly before slowly beginning to disperse. We suddenly realized these were shell bursts from anti-aircraft fire. There were about eight, the number of guns believed to be in the 88mm. battery. The disconcerting thing about them was that they were at exactly our own height, meaning that the anti-aircraft gunners had found our altitude straightaway. As the shells had burst in front, they had also observed our course correctly, so only had to reduce their estimate of the plane's speed to either hit it or damage us and the aircraft with close bursts of shrapnel. There was no merit, or future, in continuing to fly along steadily!

So, with a quick warning to Drunkie on the inter-cockpit speaking system I immediately pointed the nose steeply down and then began to weave in irregular directions—mainly away from the battery. We lost 1,500 ft. quite rapidly, then flying level at approximately 5,500, we notified H.M.S. Aurora of the reason for our brief silence and change of position. The most welcome reply was "Right, we'll change targets!" I persisted in changing direction frequently while gaining a little height. It had become obvious that the mistake in the Germans' assessment of the Swordfish's speed, in contrast to their accuracy in finding its altitude and course, had been due to their earlier experiences with the much faster Hellcats. They had not been able to distinguish clearly at the Swordfish's 7000 feet the exact type of machine and as all the others had been single-seater fighter-bombers they had set their sights for Hellcats' speed. Obviously, they would have observed the small cloud-bursts in our path and by now would have corrected their mistake—fortunate one for my observer and me. Without dallying to find out how cleverly the enemy had assessed our current position, direction, and speed, I banked the aeroplane round steeply to face the opposite compass bearing and continued to climb a little. Extra altitude would perhaps only decrease the battery's accuracy a minimal amount, but it created a slightly changing situation for them to judge and would allow more scope for another sudden large drop towards the sea if we experienced a further bursting of anti-aircraft shells uncomfortably close. More patches of grey smoke where we had been not long before and minute glitters of orange from the ground indicated that the battery was operating again, though for the moment without the initial success of the opening round. This situation might not last more than a minute or two, therefore I persisted in manoeuvring the plane on short spells in varying directions while allowing maximum periods for observing the battery area and the cruiser.

We had been informed that there would be certain time lapses between the firing of the warship's guns and the fall of shot that could be calculated. We had confirmed with the first salvo from the "Aurora" that the timespan was 25 seconds. Now a tiny flash and puff of white from the side of the cruiser signalled that a shell was on its way. At about the anticipated moment a bigger flash and cloud of dust on the ground far below showed that the shell had struck the surface. It seemed to me that the warship had been encouragingly swift in dispatching the first 'ranging' shot towards the new objective—which, of course, it could not see. By fixing the ship's position and pin-pointing the battery on a map, the gunnery officer could calculate how to direct a shell over the hills towards the target. It exploded 200 or 300 yards beyond the battery, I estimated, and just a little to the left of 'in-line'. A good start. Warrant Officer 'E' was staring at the area, apparently making up his mind what to report.

"Tell them to 'drop 200' and go right fifty", I shouted.

Drunkie did this and soon afterwards the signs of another six-inch 'brick' being fired was witnessed. Nearly half a minute later we saw the shell burst closer to the battery. We could not see the actual guns from our altitude, but we could discern the flashes they were making—indicating that they were again firing at us. Apparently, there was a duel developing between the battery intent on knocking the spotter aircraft out of the sky and the warship, with our help, hitting the anti-aircraft guns first. We were about 6000 feet again and I called to W/O 'E':

"We'll look over the other side again," and turned the Swordfish round.

About the fourth single shot landed in the 88mm. gun area and we signalled this result to the ship's gunnery officer. I was a little surprised at his response, thinking that perhaps a turret of two guns would send a pair of shells on the same trajectory.

"Sending a broadside", was his comment. This was a salvo of all six-inch guns firing simultaneously.

We watched excitedly as the row of small white-orange streaks and pale grey plumes were discharged from the "Aurora". As we waited tensely for 25 seconds to elapse, I altered course sufficiently to reduce the likelihood of being smitten by the latest batch of 88mm. missiles which we knew had just been sent upwards as more minute sparks had glittered from the appropriate location. Fortunately, we were once more out of harm's way when the missiles disintegrated into patches of grey in the sky.

Sometimes twenty-five seconds can seem quite a long period. This one concluded with greater success for the warship than had been achieved by the Germans aiming at our moving object. The 6-inch projectiles kicked up smoke and dust in, and immediately beside, the battery. It would be hard to imagine that substantial damage had not been sustained by the artillery unit, an assumption borne out by an absence of firing from the ground during several minutes of observing the region.

The ship was preparing to break from action, re-position for an attack upon other targets in the afternoon, give the gunners a short rest, await any changes in attitude from the island's garrison and assess the situation. We headed towards H.M.S. Emperor for refuelling and obtaining refreshment for ourselves. Drunkie surely was not in need of beverage. He had stressed his belief in being sufficiently inebriated to not be very aware of any demise or injury that he might suffer while aloft. As the senior officer I could have remonstrated with him or reported my concern to the executive commander but there was no need for navigation as in the clear Aegean sky we could see the carrier all the time, even if distantly at intervals, and my estimating the fall of shot positions posed no problem. A long anti-submarine patrol if remote from base, or in poor visibility, requiring a second person to concentrate on navigation while I attended to keeping the aircraft accurately on course, would definitely have proscribed heavy drinking, but in the circumstances of that flight there was little point in doing more than refraining from drinking myself and avoiding fuss. Besides, Drunkie had recently become a friend and comrade, and I was not aiming for a heroic display myself. We had been in the air 2 hours and 15 minutes in all. I entered in my logbook: *'Spotting of bombardment of battery of 88mm. guns by H.M.S. Aurora. Target straddled. Deck landing on "Emperor".'*

In the afternoon we flew off to continue spotting. Again, the gunnery personnel demonstrated their good aim and experience, reflecting good training as well as the benefit of involvement in the barrage against the Normandy coastal defences. Projectiles were hurled at various enemy positions including German headquarters and the coastal battery. The most impressive result was obtained from the further short bombardment of the 88mm. gun site. This was attacked for the second occasion to increase the chance of damaging anti-aircraft weapons remaining intact from the morning's onslaught (some may have been well protected by emplacements in the rocky terrain) and to silence them while we attended to other objectives, for there was a single flame-flash spasmodically, indicating that one or more guns were still usable.

After a smoke-shell and 'ranging' shot enabled us to direct the aim squarely at the anti-aircraft location, the gunnery officer decided to fire a salvo of several 6-inch shells—two turrets or all three. I believe the latter and, as earlier that day, we patiently counted the pause of 25 seconds after the missiles were ejected. As they struck the desired spot there sprang up a great tongue of flame and a giant eruption of blackish smoke that quickly formed an enormous column rising probably 1000 feet or more, perhaps 1,500. I judged this, estimating that the thick smoke rose about a quarter of the way towards the plane's level.

It was a remarkable sight, and from the ground must have been spectacular, though horrifying for the artillerymen or anyone else nearby. We quickly realized that an ammunition dump or fuel depot had been struck—probably the ammo supply of the battery itself. No other explanation seemed likely. It was not more than a minute or so later that the excitement and jubilation were joined by a different feeling—one of concern for casualties arising from the explosion. Pondering the matter, I regretted being connected with circumstances that almost certainly had led to deaths and injuries, even though I had not 'pulled the trigger' actually. Further reflection eventuated and I reluctantly accepted the fact that enemy gunners had been aiming at my observer and me with hostile intentions and that we were all victims of a predicament in which world events had pitted us against each other—foes who could not see each other, nor knew who the others were. I wondered how the Greek Islanders were treated by those same Germans and assumed there would be a variety of attitudes. It was known that many Islanders resented the occupation of their land and were resisting in various ways, and in some cases paying a bitter price. It would be better for everybody when the conflict was over, and we were just helping in a small way towards that end. We headed towards the escort carrier.

Later, on the 26th, I wrote the second entry of the day in my logbook: *'Spotting of bombardment of various targets for H.M.S. Aurora. One ammunition dump blown up; several fires started. Deck landing on H.M.S. Emperor. 2 hours 25 minutes.'*

On 27th October we flew twice on spotting missions for the "Aurora": of 3 hours 20 minutes and then one hour. Both were involved with bombardment of the coastal defence battery. During our second flight the warship pounded five broadsides (thirty six-inch shells) into the target area. It was understood to be a different task, as each gun had been placed in a cavity excavated out of the solid rock of the cliffs overlooking the sea, probably with a great deal of protection above and all around, with only the moderate opening in front allowing for angling the muzzle and sighting the vessels to be aimed at—probably a passage approaching from the underground for entry. It would be a lucky shot that knocked out one of these guns quickly.

There was some satisfaction in the fact, from the point of view of our side, that these guns could only fire out to sea by virtue of their protected positions in the rock and could not fire sideways or upwards. There were reported to be other cannon around the island, positioned to defend the headquarters, supply depots, etc., against troops approaching from the beaches, and such locations were the objectives of H.M.S. Aurora's gunfire on a few occasions. The ship naturally kept out of direct sight of the 5-inch coastal battery, or out of its range, using our spotting facility to inform them of their fall-of-shot, particularly when projecting the missiles over low hills which helped to obscure the cruiser from rangefinders of the enemy cannon. No doubt scouts with binoculars were positioned in hills to report the whereabouts of the ship but most of the German artillery would not have the range of the warship's guns, and apparently no reconnaissance or 'spotter' aircraft was available to them.

Another flight of 2 hours 40 minutes took place on the 28th for the purpose of spotting for H.M.S. Aurora while it bombarded three varied targets and another on the 29th of 3 hours 35 min. in which we observed for both the "Aurora" and the "Easton" while in turn they fired at gun emplacements. Targets were straddled, but the damage was unknown.

Our small force was joined by a relatively new cruiser called the "Black Prince" and after a respite of no flying on the 30th, when I was asked aboard the new vessel to discuss subsequent activities, W/O. 'E' and I again flew off the carrier on the 31st to spot for the "Black Prince". This was of 5700 tons with eight 5.25. guns (in 4 turrets) that could be angled high against air attack and had good muzzle velocity to send missiles further than comparable guns of earlier design. My logbook for that day reads: *'Bombardment spotting for H.M.S. Black Prince. Hits on gun emplacements, 6 straddles with 4-gun salvos. Deck landing on "Emperor". 2 hours 35 minutes.'*

On the flight of November 1st, we were joined by the Royal Marine, Captain Leach, so that he, too, could observe the action from the air.

H.M.S. Black Prince discharged ten salvos, all of which struck the location of the coastal defence guns. My log reads *'One direct hit believed.'*

The days following were similar, though our only passenger was Lieutenant Commander Moxey, probably of the "Aurora", who watched that vessel's bombardment on 5th. The spotting on 2nd (one hour twenty mins.) and on 3rd (four hours, our longest flight) was all for the "Black Prince". On the shorter occasion it fired ten single shots, probably for training or practice. H.M.S. Aurora reappeared on the 4th. Enemy *'gun positions straddled with several broadsides; one direct hit believed'*, was entered in my log, after flying two hours and ten minutes. Of each period in the air, some twenty minutes or more would have consisted of reaching the desired position and altitude, communicating with the ship, and waiting its readiness to begin firing. Another fifteen minutes would have been needed to return and land on the escort carrier.

From the 6th to 8th of November there were no entries in my logbook. We were returning to Alexandria Harbour, meeting officers of the other ships to discuss the cooperative efforts around Melos and giving crews rest and shore visits.

Either at Alexandria, or before arrival, we learned of the cause of the unexpectedly fierce resistance of the 1200 troops and artillerymen defending Melos. It transpired that the information secretly sent by the resistance movement had been correct and at the time the handful of warships left Alexandria the German Commander had been willing to end the war for himself and his soldiers peacefully, after perhaps a brief token refusal. Unknown to the Allies, spies in Egypt (which had plenty) had discovered the intentions of the British and as the small naval task force sailed from Alexandria, had radioed German sources in Europe. The matter was reported to Hitler who immediately selected a tough, Nazi, senior officer as Commandant to fly at once to Melos to replace the man who would have surrendered quickly—apparently, he was flown out in the same plane that took the newly appointed leader to the island. The garrison, in less than two days, was awaiting our arrival with fresh determination, either willingly or under compulsion. Doubtless those who would have preferred a quieter, quicker ending to the war that was going badly for the Nazis had little choice but to comply rather than face severe punishment from the new Commandant.

THE ATTACK ON MELOS: PART TWO
(Tony)

The Walrus (L2238) was my aircraft on 9th November when I flew off Alexandria Harbour with three Sub-Lieutenants: Vine, Davies and Wenyon, to give them radio and navigation exercises across desert landscape, and to navigate their way to Heliopolis R.A.F. Station at Cairo.

Vast stretches of sand would enable small smoke bombs to act as markers and test wind speeds and directions as though above the sea but without the drift to be calculated where any current was involved. Once near Cairo, finding the way to Heliopolis was unusually easy due to the proximity of the Pyramids, which could be seen from a considerable distance and were interesting to fly around before touching down.

The return journey was simple as I flew above the great River Nile until outskirts of "Alex", sometimes flying low, which excited a few Egyptians in little boats, rousing them from the customary drowsiness and causing them to paddle rapidly towards the bank. We had been ordered to leave the Sub-Lts.at Dekheila airfield, 12 miles along the coast from Alex, pick up Lt. Issaverdens and return to H.M.S. Emperor. After landing alongside, we were hoisted aboard. The main flying periods that day had totalled 2 hours 50 minutes; the short 'hop' from Dekheila to the harbour took 5 minutes.

A similar flight to and from Cairo and Dekheila took place the next day, again with a return to the ship.

On the 12th my assignment was to take Lieut-Commander Moxey, "Izzy", and W/O "E" from the harbour in the Walrus to Dekheila and then fly off in Swordfish 170 with Lt.-Cdr. Moxey as observer, to carry out a radio-telegraph communication test with H.M.S. King George V. Izzy later flew the Swordfish to the ship while I took Drunkie and the Lieut.-Commander back in the Walrus. Soon after our return, H.M.S. Emperor sailed again into the Mediterranean.

Thirty-seven hours later we were once more in sight of Melos and I was authorized to pilot the Swordfish again. This time Lt. Cdr. Moxey was my observer, and we were to be spotting for the battleship H.M.S. King George V.

81

The "K.G.Five", as she was called, was the first of a class of five battleships of 35,000 to 36,000 tons, being commissioned early in the war. Her ten 14-inch guns were arranged in three turrets, with four guns in the forward turret, four in the rear, and two in the second facing over the forward turret. This was an unusual arrangement, as normally only two large guns, occasionally three, were housed in one turret. Her sixteen secondary guns were of the new 5.25-inch, dual-purpose type, available for anti-aircraft defence. She had been the first battleship to be fitted with small hangars to carry two aircraft, but these were not used for that purpose by 1944 as such an important warship was seldom far from an aircraft carrier or medium cruisers carrying Walrus for reconnaissance, spotting, and anti-submarine patrol.

With the European fighting moving from the coastal bombardment phase to the northward push of armies towards Germany, Britain was beginning to transfer naval power to the Far East in anticipation of the final land and sea battles with Japan. "K.G.V" was reported to be on her way to the East, after replenishing supplies and taking on a new crew. It was seen as an opportunity to give additional practice to the crew by participating in a second, brief assault on the Melos stronghold.

Moxey and I looked down from the several thousand feet upon the coast of Melos and the sea in which the "Emperor" cruised in the distance and the "K.G.V" appeared almost below us as a tiny model. She was taking her time preparing to exercise her gunners and equipment, at a distance comfortably within the range of her big guns but believed to be beyond the limits of the German coastal battery, which was to be the target, together with the inland approaches to the emplacements.

Suddenly there appeared tiny clouds from the cliff area and moments later spouts of water leaped up from the surface of the sea on each side of the battleship. She had been straddled (but not hit) by the first salvo of several coastal guns, again demonstrating the good gunnery of the Germans. Immediately we observed a conspicuous white patch at the stern of the battleship. She had hastily *'put her rudder over'* as Moxey remarked, accelerated her propellers to increase speed, and these motions had churned the surface. The ship was turning away in the awareness of the ability of the coastal battery to reach her present position. Were the artillery pieces in the cave-like emplacements larger than reported, or was the ship just a little closer than it had calculated and just within the enemy's striking distance? I have not discovered precise answers. For the moment we were engaged in adapting to the new circumstances. *"Delay while establishing fresh position"*, was the message from the vessel. After 25 minutes, which seemed to me an unduly long period, the "K.G.V" informed us that initial shots were about to be discharged. Obviously, the battleship was of considerable importance, whereas the coastal artillery could be left at Melos without being able to affect the main war effort except for that of any vessel venturing too close to its location. Furthermore, a captain's responsibility was firstly the safety of his ship and crew in such circumstances as these. Even so, I could not help feeling that the mighty warship's personnel had taken plenty of time to reorganize.

We were told about 37 seconds would elapse between the projection of the 14-inch shell and its arrival on the island—that estimate proved to be accurate. There was no difficulty in seeing precisely where the shell contacted the rocky ground, for even at the height of the Swordfish, the 14-inch explosive threw up enough dust and debris to reveal the point of impact, though everything appeared minute. The precaution taken against the shell falling short into the sea had been too great, for it landed about 300 yards too far. Moxey and I conferred and recommended that the range be reduced 300 yards. This resulted in the second missile striking the ground only about 50 yards beyond the correct distance but two or three hundred yards to the left. We deliberated briefly and advised the warship to: *'Drop 50 and right 200'*. Lt. Cdr. Moxey was a shipborne officer (gunnery, I believe) and used to viewing bombardments from sea level, so it was useful to him to draw on the recent experience I'd had while reporting aerial observations to the cruisers, to modify or support his initial impressions from 6-7000 feet. *"The third 'brick' should drop nicely into the required area'*, we believed.

But it did not. It exploded about 200 or more yards to the left. *'Right 250'*, Moxey indicated. We watched for the next smoke signal from the muzzle of one of the K.G.V's guns, then counted 37 seconds. Again, the impact with the land was 200-250 yards to the left of where we had anticipated. Moxey and I exchanged whatever glances were possible with goggles and speaking apparatus on—it was hardly credible that the aim could have gone yet again to the left, but it had. The fact was reported by Lieut. Cdr. and a further attempt to bear the barrel further to the right was made. It seemed that the officer directing the battleship's aim was giving each team of gun layers one practice at firing its huge weapon, for in all there were ten single shots aimed at the rear approaches and supply depots associated with the coastal battery. The tendency of the explosions to

83

occur to the left of the target was repeated all through this part of the exercise. A disappointing performance, particularly after witnessing the very competent, rapid, and timely display of H.M.S. Aurora and the capable gunnery of H.M.S. Black Prince.

More heavy ammunition was used to strafe the gun emplacements in the rocky cliffs. Direct hits could not be observed but would be difficult to detect with certainty unless something like the great explosion of October 26th occurred due to the well-shielded sites of the artillery. My log-book records thirty 14-inch shells being fired that day—the later ones were probably in pairs or fours. So, the German equipment, although underground in the main, must have suffered blast-damage here and there, or severe vibration, and any radio gear above ground in the vicinity would probably have been put out of use. In any case, the assault ceased then, and the warships sailed for Alexandria, leaving the garrison on Melos to be isolated by naval power in the Aegean and by the occupation of the mainland as the Germans retreated under pressure from the British and Americans, the Russians, and the partisans. As with the troops on Crete and a few scattered islands, the Melos unit remained stranded until the Nazi surrender.

Back in harbour we learned that the gunnery officer of the "King George V" had forgotten to 'layoff' the ship's speed while adjusting aim between salvos, thus resulting in the shells repeatedly falling to the left. It was a surprising revelation—not that it had occurred once or twice, but that the persistent tendency had not alerted the officers to the cause of the fault. We hoped the comparatively unimpressive demonstration would have been greatly improved upon before the warship entered the Far Eastern conflict. There was no doubt that the one factor of 'own speed' would have made a considerable difference to effectiveness when remembered.

H.M.S. Emperor left Alexandria within a few days and anchored next at Gibraltar. It stayed only briefly. The Captain's friend Commander the Hon. David (later Lord) Cecil came aboard, and another narrative relates his joining me in the Walrus two or three days later. When Cornwall was in sight, I was authorized to fly the amphibian off the deck, report at St. Merryn Naval Air Station near Padstow and, accompanied by the Commander, proceed across country to Lee-on-Solent. It was a pleasant trip and although 29th November, the counties looked beautiful from the reasonably low altitude maintained. The aircraft was handed in for an

84

overhaul and re-location and I proceeded on a few days leave to await my next assignment.

HOMEWARD WITH SURPLUS CARGO
(Anthea)

"Home is a good place to be!"

These words were frequently heard from my mother especially when she was in her nineties, but even as far back as I can remember, whenever we'd arrive home after a holiday or weekend away, she would immediately busy herself preparing for tea—sometimes before taking off her overcoat! She and Dad would recline in comfortable chairs to sip their soothing cuppa. After all, the British understand that a good cup of tea takes care of whatever is ailing them! Mum would glance at Dad, and with a contented sigh, she'd murmur, "It's good to be home, isn't it?" To which, he would enthusiastically agree. I suspect many of us can relate—there's no place like home.

I can only imagine the unadulterated joy and anticipation of being bound for home shores after the hardships of wartime service and foreign lands. In the "Overload" account, we find Dad readying his Walrus aircraft for the flight back to England, for a welcome break after the harrowing reconnaissance missions over Melos. Nothing routine about *that* flight, as you will discover. A few surprises were in store for Tony Shipperlee.

Dad describes how the ship's captain requested his presence the day before departure and asked him to transport an interesting passenger with some unusual cargo. I'm thinking it was an honour Dad was chosen. To me it indicates the captain respected my father's flying skills and trusted him with the safety of a close friend. As you read on, you'll discover the events that transpired. Having acquainted yourself with Dad through a few of his stories, you might have gathered that Tony was a stickler for rules and regulations! You would be correct, he was—at least most of the time.

As far back as I can remember Dad set rules for me. As child, a teenager and even when I was a grown woman, he expected me to adhere to those rules, although they were unwritten. Often, to my annoyance, he would add new stipulations unexpectedly—no prior notice given, written or otherwise! As an educator he was a strict disciplinarian and I often felt he brought the school classroom atmosphere into our family home. In all fairness though, while he expected my mother and me to follow his wishes (rules) he did generally adhere to them himself. As irritating as they can be, most rules exist to protect us, or the well-being of others, don't they?

It must have been priceless to observe Dad's shocked facial expressions at seeing the size and contents of the cargo he was to transport. It would have been difficult for him to challenge a senior officer, but Lt. Shipperlee clearly knew the maximum capacity of the Walrus, and what it would safely bear so, quite in character, he would abide by, and insist upon, adhering to the safety guidelines. Obviously, he would have no desire to endanger himself, his passenger, the cargo, or the aircraft. Ending up in the drink (so to speak) would have been disastrous.

Although Tony spent many years residing away from England, he never lost the love and nostalgia for his country of birth. It was always home. He loved the exquisite beauty of the English countryside, whether he was meandering along a footpath, riding a bicycle, in a train or flying high above the patchwork of green fields. He was a lover of nature. This love for the beauty of his country inspired him to paint watercolours of Britain's fishing villages, farmsteads, steam trains, castles and rolling hills.

I find this account both amusing and heart-warming. What transpires suggests that even in wartime, the human side of people can shine forth in beautiful ways—simple ways, kind ways, like helping a friend out, enjoying the small pleasures in life, or by going out of your way to let your passenger catch a glimpse of his family estate, circling around the buildings and flying low in several passes—albeit in a Shagbat.

Yes, home matters. Kindness matters.

OVERLOAD
(Tony)

By late November 1944, the naval attack on Melos was over and our small aircraft carrier, H.M.S. Emperor was returning to Britain. It had played a key role in the engagement and was steaming to Gibraltar to unload or take on certain supplies such as fresh water and fuel, before venturing into the rough waters off the Bay of Biscay. I soon learned that at least one naval officer had joined the ship as a passenger, for a message was given to me stating that the ship's captain wanted to see me in his cabin.

"My goodness! What have I done?" I wondered, for it was seldom a four-ringed captain singled out a mere two-ringed lieutenant for a personal interview unless it was to deliver a rap over the knuckles, or for some special reason such as a signal from the Admiralty requiring the person to be transferred for urgent duties elsewhere.

The reason turned out to be quite personal. In his large private cabin, the Captain introduced me to a middle-aged man in civilian clothes, the Honourable D. Cecil, who was his personal guest. He told me this gentleman was a commander (three-ringed officer) who had been stationed at Gibraltar for a while in liaison position and had been a friend of the Captain for many years—since they were young subalterns together, I gathered. The Captain wished me to have the Honourable D. Cecil as a passenger in my Walrus seaplane when we reached England and fly him to Lea-on-Solent when I delivered the aircraft to that Fleet Air Arm base, near Portsmouth. The Commander would have some cargo to be stowed in the aircraft, but the ship's Executive Commander would attend to that the following morning. After a polite little chat, for I was 23 years old, and they were probably twice my age, I was dismissed.

The next morning, I went to the hangar to check on the servicing and loading of the aircraft and noticed large boxes being lifted into the hull behind the crew's cabin. I climbed into the Walrus and received quite a shock, for the length of the hull was occupied by wooden boxes—I think 24 in all. I tried lifting two or three and they were all heavy. Obviously, the aircraft was overloaded, and I had to do something about it. Enquiring about the crates from the ratings (junior enlisted members of the navy) who had loaded them, I learned that they contained Spanish wine, six or a dozen bottles in each. No wonder they were heavy.

88

I discussed this unexpected situation with the Petty Officer supervising the maintenance of airframes and decided to inform the Executive Commander that the load was too much for take-off from a small carrier deck. As expected, he tried to play down my fears. However, as I was the person with the experience of flying Walruses, and the guy who would be at risk if we flopped into the ocean, I persisted with my objection and then pressed to contact the Honourable D. Cecil. He was pleasant and reasonable and saw my point of view that not only would the crates of wine be lost, but our lives also if the dangerously overloaded plane could not cope with the abnormal weight. There was also the factor that some crates could work loose from the cords lashed around them in rough air conditions and press against the wires to the tail controls.

A Walrus was not designed for that type of cargo. We agreed that I should have a box weighed and use my judgment as to how many boxes could be left in the plane. Considering the modest length of the carrier's deck and other factors, I calculated that half the boxes could be left aboard the aircraft—twelve, I think. I insisted they must be carefully lashed in suitable positions, and I inspected them subsequently.

Early the following morning we were off Land's End. The "Emperor" was sailing to a refitting port beyond Cornwall, presumably preparing it for service in the Pacific campaign that was now building up. The ship's aircraft were to fly to a major F.A.A. base, probably Lee-on-Solent, but first to land at St. Merryn, a F.A.A. aerodrome near the north coast of Cornwall, to be checked by customs officers who had driven in force from Padstow. We heard that customs men were not hard on servicemen taking in a small amount of harmless goods from the Middle East but charged heavy duty if a crew member carried in, for example, several watches or leather handbags obviously for profit and not just an isolated present. They would also be looking for prohibited imports and anything threatening security. I recall placing a second leather handbag, purchased in Egypt, under my seat and parachute. In retrospect this does not seem a great idea!

All my fellow pilots, except Issaverdens, were flying the American built Hellcats, single-seat fighter bombers used around Melos recently; "Izzy" and I, being the only qualified seaplane pilots, were to fly the Walrus amphibian and Swordfish, which had been used for air-sea-rescue and "spotting" for the guns of cruisers, then the "K.G.V." One after the other the planes roared along the flight deck, and I believe the Swordfish preceded the others, about two dozen in all.

With Commander Cecil in the observer's seat of my Walrus, I turned into the wind at the stern of the deck and opened the throttle fully. Carriers normally headed into wind directly also, while their aircraft were flying off, to create the maximum wind down the deck and facilitate lift-off. With the heavy load we trundled along. The combination of strong headwind, the ship's speed, and our full power, enabled us to get the tail up, have a few tiny bounces as the plane almost lifted off the wheels and then, as we went into the open space above the bows, maintain flight and steadily gain height.

Cornwall often has fierce winds, and on this occasion, we encountered a strong one against us, so that we were slower than usual and had time to glance at the rugged coast and rural scenery. I shall always remember my emotion at once more looking down on the lovely landscape, with its typically English patchwork fields, golden Cornish beaches and tiny fishing hamlets, and cattle around farmsteads. After the constant blue sky of the Eastern Mediterranean with its hot sun fostering the wearing of shorts every day, the slightly hazy grey-blue light of late autumn brought strong hints of the colder, wetter climate. it would soon be Christmas, and we were home.

My contemplations were replaced by concentrating on the need to begin the descent and circuit around the aerodrome. As I lost height and lowered the undercarriage, I could see the Hellcats all assembled alongside the far end of the main runway. Being faster planes, and without cargo, they had reached St. Merryn well ahead of us. The fierce headwind and the load of wine crates had slowed us markedly and the effects were immediately felt again as we landed on the down-wind end of the runway, for we slowed rapidly. By the time we were halfway along the tarmac we were almost at a standstill, and I was able to turn off on a connecting taxi strip towards the control tower. The Hellcats were quite some distance away.

When the Walrus was chocked and switched off, I went up the steps of the tower to give the customary report of our arrival, while Commander Cecil decided to walk to the wardroom to see if some old friends were around. We had planned to have a light lunch and then continue our journey to Hampshire.

While I was eating a snack a few of the Hellcat pilots came in and I learned that their planes had been examined by the customs officials. It seemed that no one had enquired about the Walrus and its occupants. Perhaps our slow-moving craft, lumbering in well after the others, and quite different in appearance, had been disregarded as being nothing to do with the squadron that had just landed. I could only assume that to be the case. It was surprising they had not got us on a list. They certainly did not seem to be looking for us.

Concluding that it would be wise not to hang around but to become inconspicuous, I moved from the table and went to the bar in search of Commander Cecil. He was enjoying drinks with friends. I mentioned the situation to him and suggested that we should leave right away, and he agreed. No doubt the customs duty on dozens of bottles of wine was worth considering. Anyhow, we proceeded to the aircraft, and when the brief formalities in the control tower were over, I taxied Walrus L2238 to the runway and flew off for Hampshire.

Before reaching the New Forest area Commander Cecil told me that his family home was only a little off our flight path and asked if we could divert a few minutes to look at it from the air. It was, in fact, close to our route and we quickly found it. I was surprised to see a castle-like establishment in extensive grounds. I should not have been, for the Cecils had featured often in English history, and the present generation are descendants of William Cecil, Lord Burleigh, Minister to Queen Elizabeth 1st, and of Robert Cecil, a Prime Minister of Queen Victoria. We circled around the buildings and flew low over them before continuing to Lee-on-Solent. There the plane was handed over to a maintenance team and our personal suitcases removed.

The boxes were later unloaded and dispatched to the Commander at his expense, I believe. That evening I sampled the hoary weather of late November and travelled by train to Oxford.

ADVENTUROUS AND RESOURCEFUL
(Anthea)

The last of Tony's stories is actually one of the earlier accounts he wrote and mailed to me. I think he delighted in sharing this as the first of his WWII stories because my children were of an age to appreciate both the seriousness of the subject matter, and the fun of an "animal" story that captured their imagination and held their attention. It was so like my father to use stories to teach children. Whether it was in the classroom where he taught, or in a chair with a grandchild sitting on his knee, or across the table from him as they grew up, he captured their full attention. His grandchildren could never hear enough of his stories.

It's no wonder he excelled in this area for he had been an avid reader since a boy and especially loved adventure stories. He sought out books that captured his imagination, stories with strong characters who stood for good and fought off evil. As a boy he enjoyed Robin Hood books, King Arthur and the Knights, anything about animals, or the Wild West. Avid readers are often excellent writers and storytellers.

I suspect that he developed his adventurous spirit from heroes in such books. It must be evident by now that Tony Shipperlee had a daring side, and he loved the exhilaration of flying aircraft. He confided in me several times that while he was never one to make stupid mistakes or court unnecessary danger, he had taken a few calculated risks. My dad possessed a certain swagger as a young man. Some of his flying stories have not been written down but they have been relayed to family members and friends. What I remember so well is how his face would light up when he spoke of flying low over the Pyramids in Egypt, or when he nostalgically described circling Stonehenge on a moonlit night. My favourite tale is how animated and excited he became as he chuckled mischievously about flying under the Firth of Forth Bridge in Scotland.

The Otter that Emulated a Porpoise illustrates that my father was a man of courage and tenacity, but also one who could think and act quickly out of the box. He was amazingly resourceful. I chuckle as I recall the number of rolls of masking tape we discovered in his study as we dealt with a house full of belongings after he passed away. I kid you not, he could literally work wonders with it—he could fix or construct anything with his supply of sticky paper. It was a source of amusement to our family, and particularly the grandchildren, one of whom took photographs of all the masking tape fixes found in and around his house. With tongue in cheek, I wonder if a few rolls of masking tape might have come in handy, had he it as a resource in the following story?

I hope you have enjoyed reading my father's accounts of his WWII escapades. No doubt his experiences will have given you a glimpse into a time when world war ravaged the globe. Long may peace reign. Perhaps the expansion chapters I wrote have provided an additional perspective into the memoirs of Lt. John Anthony Shipperlee. I hope you have captured the essence of the man everyone loved and knew as Tony.

Of course, to me he will always be my beloved Dad.

THE OTTER THAT EMULATED A PORPOISE

(Tony)

By July 1945 only a few months of my naval service remained, for the European war had ended several weeks previously and Japan was to surrender in August. I had carried out the second series of deck landing trials of the Sea Otter amphibian airplane aboard H. M. S. "Pretoria Castle" and was temporarily at a 'rest' posting in a communications flight at Ayr, on the south-west coast of Scotland. This consisted of flying a variety of aircraft on duties that also varied from day to day.

On the 13th I was assigned to Sea Otter No. 878 for the duty of landing in the sea off Largs, about thirty miles north, to pick up a young pilot, Sub-Lieutenant Jones, and give him his first instruction in flying seaplane. He was already a trained pilot on land-based machines. He would be rowed out from the jetty and would rendezvous with me some 150 yards seawards. At the prearranged time I alighted in the Sea Otter about 300 yards from the shore and taxied towards the small boats moored some fifty yards from the beach. A fisherman rowed one of these in my direction and a young naval officer stood up and waved. I throttled back so the engine merely ticked over, enabling the oarsman easily to guide his little craft to the side of the flying boat.

The young pilot clambered aboard and took his seat in the co-pilot's position. In the Sea Otter, as in a Walrus, the pilot's and observer's seats were side by side, with a duplicate set of controls often fitted so that a second pilot could operate when a particular purpose required this. My early seaplane/amphibian flying training in Poole Harbour had been acquired mainly in dual-controlled walruses.

Sub-Lieut. Jones seemed a pleasant young man. He was keen to convert to the small flying-boats. This opportunity was in fact a privilege as only 8 percent approximately of Fleet Air Arm pilots ever received training on seaplanes. The great majority were confined to landplanes (though often landing these on carrier decks) for in comparison there were so few floatplanes. We taxied around the deep off-shore water for about ten minutes while I explained various points concerning taking off and landing in this sea compared with doing so on runways, showing him the controls, and allowing him to try manoeuvring the plane on the water surface. Then we positioned ourselves downwind of a long stretch of open sea to obtain a good run clear of any boats.

The programme was to consist firstly of a demonstration take-off by me, enabling the pilot under instruction to observe the procedures and hear a commentary, and experience the sensation of rushing through water like a speedboat but with quite different handling qualities. Later he would handle the controls with me and feel the movement of the aircraft as it left the water and gently steer it in the air. After two or three 'dual' take-offs he would be able to try it unaided; then begin to receive guidance in landing, at first under ideal conditions, in due course under conditions of stronger winds and rougher water. Probably his instruction period would last three weeks or more and be given by two or three different pilots of suitable experience. But for this initial occasion he would need to get the general impression of the difference between taking off from water and from land.

So, I turned the aircraft into wind and opened the throttle steadily until we were racing through the sea on full power. The hull rose in the water as usual with the two wing-floats out of the sea most of the time, only in contact with it when moderate waves rose to splash against them. The sea was not a rough one, but its waves were sufficiently choppy to allow a demonstration of a typical take-off in good conditions. Thus far, all proceeded normally, and like the many earlier occasions in my experience. We had gained about eighty percent of the speed required for lift-off and in a few more seconds we should hear that lovely "hiss" as they rose to the very top of the sea and the ridge under its centre cut 'V' along the water for a couple of hundred yards until we were fully airborne. This would probably occur at 52-55 knots—approximately 62 m.p.h.

We had reached about 46 knots when there was a sudden and alarming crash behind our seats and the plane shuddered very slightly. For a moment I thought some submerged object had struck the hull. On glancing over my shoulder, I could hardly believe the sight of the camera hatch being swept backwards along the hull floor by a fierce jet of water. The camera hatch was a circular device of 10 to 12 inches diameter that was screw-twisted or otherwise fastened into the opening in the base of the hull, only removed in flight to enable an aerial camera to be fitted into the opening for photographing downwards. The airframes mechanic responsible for the signing of the inspection certificate this day had obviously not carried out this part of the duty thoroughly. Never before had this happened to me, nor to anyone I knew.

My instant reaction was to throttle back and stop the ten inch wide jet of sea gushing into the hull; but even as my hand instinctively reached out to the throttle, other realizations flashed into my mind, for here was a real emergency—if I stopped the aircraft there would be no likelihood of our retrieving the hatch from the tail of the hull and getting it back in place, let alone twisting it round to fully close it, before the water had entered in sufficient quantity to cause the plane to start sinking. We were now too far from the boats and shore to swim comfortably, and an adverse tide could wash us well out of the area. In any case the sinking of the comparatively new aircraft, whilst not blamed on me, would automatically result in a court of enquiry to ascertain the cause and following actions of all concerned. A trail of investigations would ensue, with naval court formalities and the other unpleasant procedures that surround such enquiries. The alternative was to continue at full speed, despite accelerating the entry of the mass of water, and to hope that by some miraculous combination of engine power, wing-lift and wind, we would rise above the sea before it swamped the aircraft's interior.

These contradictory thoughts flashed through my brain in what must have been only a second or two, and as I clasped the throttle lever, I decided to leave the engine at full power for a few more moments and judge whether to take the second, but more dangerous, alternative—for stopping would certainly mean sinking or at best being waterlogged to such an extent that the plane would be inoperable and would slowly submerge anyway. At least the more spectacular choice would maybe have a chance of success. The next few seconds would indicate the probability or otherwise.

The great jet of salt-water continued to thunder into the hull like several firemen's hoses combined into one. It entered with frightening velocity as we raced along the sea like a powerboat in a competition. For two or three seconds we gained just a little more speed and I calculated that we must be near to normal take-off speed, though with the weight of water we would need extra speed. Then it seemed as though the mass of water already in the hull (by now 6 to 8 inches deep) and the resistance caused by the opening against the sea, were becoming too much for the plane and I sensed that we were not rising noticeably any further. We careered along the surface with the small waves buffeting the wing-floats and the hull being on the point of easing above the sea's face—yet not quite managing to do so. Time, of course, was against us for every moment more of the salty liquid poured into the plane.

This uncertain state continued for a period that seemed like minutes but could not have been. The needle reached normal take-off speed on the indicator but lost momentum to increase at the normal rate and we were only maintaining our situation against the increasing weight of water and the pressure against the open hatch. Within moments we would reach the awful stage when the plane would be forced lower in the sea and we would have to climb onto the wings with engine switched off, for the position of the engine and propeller, high in the wings, would pull the aircraft over when the drag of the hull became too great.

On several previous occasions when inadvertently landing in water with wheels down (instead of retracted into the wings) small flying boats, in particular Walruses, had turned upside down and occupants killed. An age of apprehension ensued during those endless seconds. Small waves were jolting the hull an inch or so above the water and back into it, then the moments of being out of the water lengthened and suddenly we were fully clear of the sea—by only inches. The plane, weighed down by many gallons of liquid, could not gain height and I realized that somehow the quantity of liquid had to be reduced. We had cleared ourselves from the ocean's grip by only a minimal margin, so I kept the throttle at full power and held the plane level just above the sea. Gravity began pulling some of the water out through the hole. We continued like this for perhaps half a minute, trailing spray from the camera hatch as the rush of air past the outside helped to suck the unwelcomed liquid out. My breath returned and I felt reassured. Unfortunately, however, our troubles were not over, as an unforeseen phenomenon came into being.

Once the seaplane was free of the resistance of the ocean, and the escaping water began to reduce the abnormal weight, the speed started to improve. I was building up the knots in preparation for gaining height. But the fluid nature of the water caused our improving acceleration to press the water back towards the rear and in moments all of it was in the rear half of the plane. This weighed the tail down so that we were becoming nose up and tail close to striking the sea. I pushed forward hard on the control column, but it hardly moved for the abnormal liquid cargo was extremely heavy at the back. Forcing my shoulders against the seat I stretched out my arms as strongly as I could while pushing on the lower part of the column with my legs. The control moved only slowly, grudgingly resisting my efforts, but it did gradually yield, and we sluggishly regained a level position without the underbelly touching the sea. But then the next stage in this drama occurred.

As the posture of the plane changed from tail down to horizontal, the water surged forward to spread itself along the hull, causing the nose to depress and increase the forward momentum of liquid, so the tail rose and we were quickly, at an alarming angle, aiming down towards the sea. A struggle with the control column was again involved but this time to raise the nose so that we did not dive into the ocean. Much force was needed to level the aircraft but gradually this was achieved.

Of course, as the plane assumed the correct altitude, the tendency of the water to rush towards the stern occurred again but now I was anticipating it and prepared to force the column forward a little sooner so that the threat of stalling in the tail-down position was decreased slightly, though the hazardous posture still occurred to an unpleasant extent. We suffered the forward and backward flow of the water several more times with its effect on the aircraft. Flying it was more like trying to control a horse rearing on its hindlegs one moment and then putting down its head and kicking up its back legs the next. Nevertheless, the aircraft was flying increasingly higher as the stream of water from the hatch hole briefly accelerated each time the forward and backward flow alternated, making this ballast ever lighter. Our porpoise-like manoeuvres became less violent and were gently coaxing portions of the remaining inch of water through the opening. This see-sawing was enacted along about a mile of open sea. Had anyone from a boat or shore been watching through binoculars our performance must have appeared remarkably peculiar.

By now we could fly normally and, after building up speed and height, we headed back to base, with the remnants of the water dripping from the hatch in occasional spots. I did not initiate disciplinary action against the mechanic involved, and of course he claimed he had noticed no undue looseness in the hatch at the time of his inspection, but I did instruct the Petty Officer to check this mechanic from time to time and the camera hatches also.

The rather white-faced Sub. Lt. Jones said little on our way to Ayr. The poor fellow's first seaplane flight must have been imprinted on his mind for some while. He had certainly had a frightening experience and I don't know whether he overcame the reaction and later asked for further instruction, for my flight next morning and for several days was in a two-seater Firefly fighter, further afield in Northern Ireland, Yorkshire and to the other coast of Scotland, and after that to the North-East of Scotland.

I just had to *presume* that Sub. Lt. Jones was reassured that camera hatches rarely flew out of position and that his ambition to fly floatplanes remained strong. I would never know for certain though, for while I was in Northern Scotland, the atom bomb was dropped on Japan, and I was transferred to the South of England, and I was soon awaiting demobilization.

EPILOGUE
(Anthea)

John Anthony Shipperlee, who was nicknamed "Tony", was born in Leigh-on-sea, Essex, on 12th January 1921. He was an only-child with an enthusiastic and adventurous spirit, whose loving parents encouraged him to play the piano, sing in the boys' choir and join the boy scouts, where he was a drummer in the band and participated in numerous Drumhead parades in the Oxford area. Athletically inclined, his favourite sport at Southfield School was rugby and he was also an avid train spotter, but his artistic talent was undeniable. He loved to draw, and he was rarely without a sketch pad, or far from his easel and paints.

Shortly after the start of WWII, Tony was selected to the Fleet Air Arm branch of The Royal Navy, where in 1941 he reported for training at a shore station called H.M.S. St. Vincent, followed by naval officer training at The Royal Naval College, Greenwich. Lieutenant Shipperlee received advanced training at Crail in Scotland, piloting a Fairey Swordfish, a naval torpedo-bomb dropper, and subsequently was ordered to report to The Royal Motor Yacht Club in Sandbanks, for night flying and additional sea plane training on the Walrus. During his service Tony flew a total of 14 types of aircraft including the Spitfire, Firefly and Sea Otter. During the Arctic Convoy of WWII, he embarked in H.M.S. Sheffield, and as a Walrus pilot he catapulted off numerous times to carry out wartime duties. He loved take-off and landing, and his many stories are always compelling and sometimes humorous. He was awarded 5 campaign medals for distinguished wartime service, and in 2012 received number 6, the Arctic Star.

While stationed in Arbroath, Tony met his future wife, Phyllis Slack who was serving in the WRNS. The two were a great match (in Tony's words) so he proposed after only a few months and Phyllis accepted. The two were married in November 1943, and Anthea arrived in 1945. A few months later Tony was demobbed, and after completing an accelerated teacher training course, he accepted a position in Oxford as art and crafts teacher in a secondary school, during which time he authored a published book entitled "Your Book of Lino Cutting".

Tony's adventurous spirit resulted in a three-year teaching contract that took his family to East Africa, where Tony was Headmaster of the Victoria Nile Primary School in Jinja, Uganda. The equator climate was ideal for outdoor activities, so the family enjoyed an active social life and experienced many exciting adventures among the African wildlife. Tony loved wild animals and eagerly captured photographs of the majestic wild animals in their natural habitats.

Two years after returning to be headmaster of a primary school in Oxfordshire, Tony's yearning for new adventures precipitated another move ... to Sydney Australia, where he and Phyllis resided for 31 fulfilling years. He first taught in a primary school in Sydney and later, after persevering through a 4-year art course at Sydney University, he graduated top of his class, securing a degree in art, which opened the door to a position as Senior Lecturer of the art and craft department at Wollongong Teacher Training College, before retiring in 1995 to settle here in Dorset. Suffice it to say that his wanderlust prevailed so besides regular trips to see Anthea, Chuck, and family in the U.S., he and Phyllis enjoyed extended holidays in Canada, New Zealand, and the Mediterranean.

Tony was one of the most multi-talented, skilled, and purpose-driven individuals—a one of a kind. Whatever he chose to do, he not only did it well, but to perfection—and with great passion and enthusiasm, always giving 100% of his energy. His natural ability for drawing and painting enabled him to produce beautiful water colours, pastels, and oil paintings, which he did from inspiration and for the sheer joy of creating something of beauty. With skilled fingers and a lump of clay on a potter's wheel, he could create a remarkable piece of pottery, glazed in one of his own glazes and fired in the brick kiln that he built!

Tony will be remembered for his lasting impact on this earth. He was blessed with the God-given gifts of teaching others through lively conversation and by sharing compelling stories of great interest. He would command an audience in the most unassuming and humble manner, sometimes even self-deprecating, and had the ability to teach others, without them realizing they were learning! He shared those valuable gifts with everyone he met throughout his life, right up until his last day. Whether grandchild, friend, or complete stranger, an encounter with Tony's unique and charming way of being authentically himself, left a profound and lasting impression.

Love for and loyalty to family was evidenced in his acts of devotion to Phyllis, his beloved wife and soul mate of 71 years. Despite his own age and physical constraints, he cared for her himself and when he was unable, he provided continuous care for her until she passed away at home in 2015. Despite the magnitude of the loss, he doggedly forced himself, in his own words, "to struggle on". His bravery in WWII was only surpassed by his courage in the face of recent challenges. Despite his declining physical strength, his brilliant mind was incredibly intact, his attention to detail impeccable, and he could disarm you with a mischievous, boyish grin, or make you giggle with his quirky sense of humour. He never stopped imparting knowledge and continued to share enthralling stories you never wanted to end. His love for Anthea and family was expressed in a daily phone call initiated by him or received from Anthea. Right up until the day he passed, he enjoyed visits and outings with friends and neighbours, and he loved his dedicated and compassionate team of carers, whom he considered his friends.

Tony will be greatly missed by Anthea and Chuck, his 3 grandchildren, David, Stephen, and Chandra, his great-grandchildren, and many others whose lives he touched. Those who knew and loved him rejoice and celebrate his 97 amazing years of living life out loud. His legacy lives on in his paintings, his stories and through his inspirational example of living life with enthusiasm and purpose.

MEMORABILIA GALLERY

Black & White Photographs of Original Oil Paintings

by J.A. Shipperlee

Planes and Trains of WWII Era

Walrus Z1761 Flying near its
Ship H.M.S. Sheffield

Sea Otter deck landing of
H.M.S. Pretoria Castle

Hurricane aircraft flying over
England

H.M.S. Sheffield and Convoy

City of Coventry Locomotive
46240

Somerset & Dorset Locomotive
40654

Carrying out deck landing trials
in Sea Otter JM 945 on flightdeck
of H.M.S. Pretoria Castle, off the
Isle of Arran, February, 1945, to
test the maximum load that could
be taken off and landed aboard a
modest sized carrier prior to the
use of Sea Otters in the Far East
conflict. Film made for Admiralty
and recommendations for slight
modification of aircraft ailerons
and trim tabs; carried out by
Vickers-Supermarine at High Post.

Photograph from Tony's album,
showing Sea Otter landing on
H.M.S. Pretoria Castle, with his

Tony at Netheravon Intermediate
Training. Summer 1941. Fairey
Battle Aircraft.

In training beside Tiger Moth Aircraft at Elmdon 1941.

In the cockpit of Swordfish HS 170 on flight deck of H.M.S. Emperor. Safe landing after reconnaissance over Melos. Tony's handwritten note on back of photo reads: "*Taken by ship's photographer after we'd 'landed on' deck from a 4-hour flight on Nov 3, over Melos. 'Gadget' in the observer's hand in the foreground is an aerial camera— we found it useful at times! Pity we were in an old 'stringbag' at the time, but I suppose we can't be lucky every time, in the way of comfort.*"

Tony with Fulmar Aircraft

Tony about to fly off deck of H.M.S. Emperor in Swordfish 170, Sept- Nov 1944, to perform reconnaissance over Melos

2008 at the Fleet Air Arm Museum beside a Supermarine Walrus.

Photo Credits:
David Tripp, who captured the photograph during a tour of the
museum, led by his grandfather, Tony Shipperlee, at the Royal Naval
Air Station (RNAS) Yeovilton, UK.

Picture of an original leaflet (in German) dropped
over Melos.

English translation of the leaflets dropped over Melos
encouraging German soldiers to surrender.

The WWII medals awarded to J. A. Shipperlee.

108

Photograph of a page from Tony's log book
referencing observations from reconnaissance
flights over Melos.

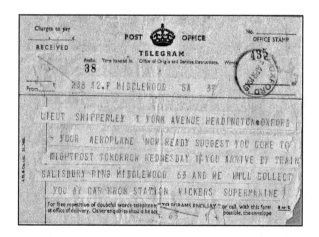

Telegram received by Tony at his parent's home in
Oxford after Supermarines had carried out modifications
on the Sea Otter resulting from his report after the first
sessions of trial landings.

Viewed from the bridge—a mighty wave crashes over the
bows of H.M.S. Sheffield.

The largest waves after the storm reached height
measuring over 70 feet.

Photo credits of the storm go to the ship's photographer
(name unknown) on board H.M.S Sheffield in February
1943. All photos of the seas were taken after the cyclone
as the mist and sky were clearing a day or so later; it was
impossible for the ship's photographer to take pictures
during the storm itself—too dangerous as the spray and
mist flying above the water prevented anything from
being seen. This image shows the fate shared by most of
the ship's boats.

111

H.M.S. Sheffield Arctic Convoy, February 1943

Ο Τζων Σέπερλη, πιλότος σε αναγνωριστικό αεροπλάνο του στόλου που έκανε τον κανονισμό βολής των πυροβόλων των αγγλικών πλοίων τα οποία βομβάρδιζαν την Μήλο το 1944.

A photograph of page 293 in the book about German occupation in Greece, by Gregory Belivanakis. The book title in English is *The German in Milos in 1941-1945.* My father provided the photograph of himself for the book.

Acknowledgement to **Dany Cheij** who translated the caption as follows: "John Shipperlee, pilot on reconnaissance aircraft of the fleet that made the rules of firing of the cannons from the English ships that bombed Milos in 1944."

AIRCRAFT	ENGINE
D.H. TIGER MOTH	GIPSY MAJOR *
BATTLE #	MERLIN II
SWORDFISH	PEGASUS III
ALBACORE	TAURUS II
OXFORD (TWIN)	2 CHEETAH X
WALRUS I & II ⊙	PEGASUS VI
SEAFOX	NAPIER RAPIER
FULMAR II	MERLIN XXX
RELIANT	LYCOMING
SEA OTTER	MERCURY XXX
SEAFIRE L III ✕	MERLIN 55M
TRAVELLER	WASP JUNIOR
FIREFLY φ	GRIFFON II **
AUSTER	CIRRUS MINOR

* The smallest engine, 130 Horse-power, on the
elementary training plane.
** The most powerful, 1,730 H.P.
# Most intermediate & advanced training done on
these; 4 months.
⊙ More hours on these amphibians than any other A/c.
✕ Spitfire with deck-hook. φ More on these later in war.

A list of the aircraft flown by Lieutenant John A.
Shipperlee during the years 1941-1945.

H.M.S. Emperor September-November 1944